Praises

The funeral eulogy is to some degree a final "report card" of the life we lived. Kian Dwyer has given us in her enlightening book, *Living Your Chosen Eulogy*, the formula to achieve a better grade.

Dennis H. Jandt
President, Jandt Funeral Homes

Kian's personal story is so timely for this moment in history.

Brad Walton, WCCO-CBS/Infinity
Author of *How Does the Heart Know Love?*

One of the most interesting interviews I have done in my 35 years at the mic.

Kevin Doran, WLEA 1480AM, New York

Living Your Chosen Eulogy is a must read for individuals who are searching for a deeper connection to the Universe and want a life filled with reverence, joy, and love. A highly recommended book!

USA Book News

Living Your Chosen Eulogy is a gripping book with a unique concept which redefines kindness in a world that takes gratitude for granted. Kian Dwyer is a leader motivating others to take charge of their lives based on their inner values, beliefs, and moral compass. In so doing, they are able to choose their own unique eulogy and live by those standards every day. Dwyer's incredible insight is much needed in today's world.

Dan McCormick President and CEO: Grand Itasca
Clinic and Hospital, Grand Rapids, MN

Each one of us will take the life path we need to walk to grow. This book is but a tool to help ease the burden for people who are looking for some piece to their life puzzle to move forward. I can say without hesitation that those who seem to resonate with this book will find that it will help them take the leap into celebrating life to a much higher degree and in the process help all those whom they come in contact with!

Kristen Brown, Ph.D.
International/Intercultural Education

CAUTION—If you read this book you will have to buy many more copies to give to others. It's what the book is about—how to give to yourself by giving to others.

Richard J. Obershaw, MSW, LICSW, ACSW
Director and Founder: Grief Center, Burnsville, MN
Author of *Cry Until You Laugh*

We could all use more "positive energy." That is my New Year's resolution—to live each day like it is my last, so that I have no excuse not to be happy.

Jennifer Smith

I just wanted to thank you for writing such an inspiring book. It is one of those works that is deceptively simple and very powerful at the same time. I've read it twice; putting it into practice will take a lifetime. I expect the practicing will be transforming.

Jeanne Schwartz

I have read most of your book and enjoy it immensely. I especially like the way that you have woven your personal life story into your encouraging statements which are designed to help us all make this a better world for ourselves and those around us.

Ann Maland

I'm very impressed. I found the book to be very settling and reaffirming to our true purpose: our inner power is meant to be positive. The book is easy to relate to and offers tools of support and well-written words of encouragement for self-discovery. The book was hard to put down. *Living Your Chosen Eulogy* acts as a roadmap for people: to practice living life with conviction, to desire to take the next step, to start living life with reverence. This vertical path creates harmony far beyond one's self. Kian Dwyer's book is an easy read for all walks of life!

Dan Barrett AFL-CIO Local 149

Kian, it was a great pleasure to have you as a guest on "Plain Talk." I believe your insights brought a better understanding to the listeners about the cultural differences between our country and the Middle East. You're a great guest and I hope your book does well. Your story is unique and one that brings hope.

Brad Dehmlow, host of "Plain Talk," KLFD

I enjoyed reading about "The Dash" and "The Room." Even though I've read a number of self-help books over the years, I was not familiar with either of those writings. I learned from my Mom to live in the present and to make each day a masterpiece, but I still struggle with this. Thanks for all your references and helpful reminders.

Bonnie Harma

We're very happy with the increase in our listenership and making the top 10 in the Twin Cities in this last Arbitron. With relevant subject matter and great guests like yourself, I know we can keep our ratings up.

Darci Keen, Producer—FM107 WFMP Ian Punnett Show M-F mornings 5-9

I was touched by your own personal eulogy included in the book, and you have inspired me to write my own. Thank you for sharing from deep within your heart and challenging each of us to help make the world a better place by living from our own authentic self. There is much to celebrate in this joyous journey through life.

Joy Kuby, Author of
The Fortunate Four & Other Journeys of the Heart

Kian Dwyer's ever-present smile brightens my day. She brings a freshness that renews my spirit, especially on those days when the workload threatens to drag me down. Kian is gentle with the children and possesses an instinctive insight into ways to redirect those with even the most challenging behaviors. As Kian 'lives her chosen eulogy' among us, we are the beneficiaries.

Stephanie R. Gustafson
Director/Teacher: Christ Church Preschool Learning Center, Minneapolis, MN

You really are one of my heroes you know. You are a good example to follow, you wonderful spirit! Thank you for filling me with your tenacity and ability to see far!

Kerry Beck

I love ya gal and see you're touching people all over the place. Yahooooooooooo!

Beth Kramer

Living
Your Chosen Eulogy

live
today
how you
want
to be
remembered

Happy Birthday Kala,

Celebrate the gifts we each bring on this spirited journey through Life!

Kim Kruger
2007

Living
Your Chosen Eulogy

live
today
how you
want
to be
remembered

Kian K. Dwyer

Beaver's Pond Press, Inc.
Edina, Minnesota

Author's Note: Some of the names and identifying details of people described in this book have been changed to preserve confidentiality.

Excerpts from *I Kissed Dating Goodbye* © 1995, 2003 by Joshua Harris. Used by permission of Multnomah Publishers, Inc.

The Dash poem, © 1996, Linda Ellis, Linda's Lyrics, *www.lindaslyrics.com* used by permission.

Excerpts of *Transitions* are © Julia Cameron and used by permission.

Surprise.com used by permission.

Peace Pilgrim: Her Life and Work in her Own Words © 1982, 1991 Friends of Peace Pilgrim. An Ocean Tree Book and used by permission.

ISBN 1-59298-097-X

Library of Congress Catalog Number: 2005920260

Book design and typesetting: Mori Studio
Cover design: Mori Studio

Printed in the United States of America

First Printing: February 2005

07 06 05 04   6 5 4 3 2 1

First Edition Printed January 2004

Beaver's Pond Press, Inc.   7104 Ohms Lane, Suite 216
Edina, MN 55439
(952) 829-8818
www.BeaversPondPress.com

If your favorite bookstore doesn't carry this book you can place orders through *www.BookHouseFulfillment.com* or call 1-800-901-3480. Reseller discounts available.

We are each as unique as the formation of a melting candle.

Follow your heart's desire to live life with purpose and meaning based on your core values.

—Kian Dwyer

Dedication...

To a woman who called herself "Peace Pilgrim" from 1953 to 1981. Peace Pilgrim walked more than 25,000 miles on a personal pilgrimage for peace. She vowed to "remain a wanderer until mankind has learned the way of peace, walking until given shelter and fasting until given food." In the course of her 28 year pilgrimage she touched the hearts, minds, and lives of thousands of individuals all across North America. Her message was both simple and profound. It continues to inspire people all over the world. It has transformed me and I include in this book, passages from her "Steps Toward Inner Peace" booklet for your enjoyment.

> *This is the way of peace: overcome evil with good, and falsehood with truth, and hatred with love.*
>
> *—Peace Pilgrim*

To my mother, whom I can see has truly chosen me to be her daughter and who, through adoption, has given me a most meaningful and fulfilling life. I am forever grateful.

Contents

Foreword

Living Your Chosen Eulogy is about living your life to its fullest NOW without regrets. It explains how to make a difference "your" way during the post 9/11 era, inspiring you to live your own life with meaning, gratitude, and love. This book guides you toward redefining yourself for a new dynamic life—a life based on positive choices, integrity, and living with purpose and intention. These choices come from our own set of beliefs, values, talents, and skills. The message woven throughout the pages shows how celebrating the gifts we each bring on this spirited journey will better our own lives as well as the lives of others in America and over the world.

Living Your Chosen Eulogy gives us the tools to live today how we want to be remembered. It explains that we may not be able to solve the world's problems but we can control ourselves and our own thoughts and actions. By improving our thoughts and actions we can influence those immediately around us and transform the world one step at a time. There is goodness within all of us. Or, the potential to be and do good—it's a choice we make. We can discover what our true gifts and talents are by not complicating life. Sometimes our true skills, natural abilities, and what we're good at (the obvious) is hard to see. Simple exercises presented throughout this book will help us find our natural abilities.

The 9/11 tragedy is imprinted in our minds. We persevered through the 2004 presidential election. The Tsunami wave disaster death toll reached an estimated 150,000 plus. Now what? Here's a book about uniting people and the world by simply "showing up," living today how you want to be remembered in the end. Think about the eulogy you would want your best friend or family to read about you.

How will we bridge the gap? How can we live from love rather than from fear and anger? How can we make a difference in this world?

I believe that in order to have kindness and peace in the world we must first be kind and peaceful ourselves. Throughout these pages you will be moved toward inner peace, joy, and compassion. When you feel this deep within, you'll emanate joy and peace. And then you'll see joy and peace around you and in the world.

Living Your Chosen Eulogy is a universal book which doesn't focus on any specific religion. After all, that would create division. Author Wayne Dyer says, "Organized religion divides us whereas spirituality unites us." The first edition of *Living Your Chosen Eulogy* created some controversy. Perhaps it's the negative feeling some readers place on the word "eulogy." Some think the book is about preparing for the end. Rather it's about living your best life now. Some tie the word "eulogy" to church and think it's a religious term and that I am pushing my religion on them. A eulogy is a tribute, not a religious term. Some look through the book not seeing scriptures and say it's not religious enough. *Living Your Chosen Eulogy* is simply a motivational guide helping us live from our inner goodness to create our best lives. This brings forth a positive outlook creating a chain reaction to improve the world.

There will be references to different religious groups based on my experiences. I do not tell people to join any one group in order to have a purpose. I believe that we can learn something from the religions of the world. I feel by being open-minded to other opinions, our own beliefs and values become stronger. Most religions offer the basic message of being a good person. There is the potential for everyone to be good...it's a choice we can make.

I was one of only four children ever adopted by an American family from strife-ridden Iran. The majority of Iranians are of the Muslim faith. There are no records of any of my biological family and I was not born in a hospital so one cannot say definitively that I was Muslim. I was raised Catholic and went to a Lutheran college. I don't believe in labeling and to this day I don't say "I'm Catholic or I'm Lutheran," just as I don't say "I'm Republican or I'm Democrat." I don't put bumper stickers on my car. I once heard minister and radio talk show host Ian Punnett say that he doesn't wear a cross. He said, "If people cannot tell who I am by how I act then what good is a cross, a bumper sticker, or a Christian symbol on my car?"

Living Your Chosen Eulogy is a resource to help you develop intentional choices of positive actions rather than angry reactions. We have the power to control our actions and focus on what selfless acts we can do in our own community. When we concentrate on the baby steps we can take and on what we each can do with our own gifts, our community, country, and world become a much healthier place to live.

Introduction

Think about your life. The camera is rolling, following you like a shadow in your home, your workplace, while you're shopping, running errands, socializing with friends, or gathering with family. Picture yourself as if you're watching a movie. Who are you? What's your character? Are you proud of who you are? If your life were a movie how would your character be perceived?

Many of us live day after day, wondering about our purpose in the world. We are unconscious of the possibilities within us and before us. *Living Your Chosen Eulogy* means choosing to live your most authentic, honorable self—first through words and then through actions.

Your soul has chosen a personality for Earth. It has lessons to learn and gifts to teach others, just as mine has learned and is teaching. It is up to you to connect with your soul to cultivate the awareness of your higher self. To do this, you need to follow your heart and inner wisdom up the ladder of conscious choices to a better life. A life of clarity and creativity is one for which your inner spirit longs. When you give out of kindness and the goodness of your heart, you will move up the vertical path in abundance and joy, void of pain. You will learn to trust your heart and go with your intuition or inner voice.

Conscious living with intention and radiance brings forth your chosen eulogy. When you understand and accept death (that in the end we all pass), then you become conscious of living and can focus fully on your purpose in the universe without fear. When you let go of fear and let your heart and soul guide you, you will be amazed at what you can accomplish. More importantly, you'll transmit euphoria that will create a chain reaction of positive energy. This energy contributes to the evolution of you, others, and the world.

Living Your Chosen Eulogy is a positive, motivational book along the lines of Wayne Dyer, Cheryl Richardson, or Dr. Phil. It encapsulates twenty years of some of the works and words of the best self-help authors and melds them with my own concepts and philosophy. *Living Your Chosen Eulogy* helps you see your own unique gifts and helps you show those gifts so that others will show theirs. This ripple effect automatically improves the world.

This book will show you how to connect with your soul. You will be able to learn through love and wisdom versus doubt and fear. The "right" way, the truth comes from within you, and you will be empowered to live your very own unique eulogy.

A eulogy is a tribute (high praise) showing respect, gratitude, or affection. It's something that extols the worth, virtue, or effectiveness of the person. In the traditional sense, a eulogy is a written expression in praise of another person which is presented at his or her funeral or memorial service. Alternatively, I look at it as a celebration of one's life. Or, as described in my book, it can be something you've chosen to write as a commitment to carry out your true values which come from your heart and soul. *Living Your Chosen Eulogy* is choosing to live as your most honorable self every day, starting now.

The title, *Living Eulogy* first came to mind after my grandmother's death in April, 2000. I remember my mother saying of my grandmother, "She was a real classy lady." Almost 92 years of an incredible lady made a deep impact on my mother's life. Then, in April, 2003, came my grandfather's funeral. I had visited him in a nursing home every week for several years. Following his funeral, the title *Living Eulogy* popped up in my mind again.

It's interesting how a funeral makes us suddenly aware of the preciousness of time. Our love exudes as we connect with family and friends, promising to stay in touch more often.

This book is not about self-help but world-help, putting your **best** authentic self forward to better our world. It is not about the weakest link but about being your **best** strongest link in a chain with other leaders. This chain reaction provides the means to creating a community, state, country and world of kindness.

Living Your Chosen Eulogy shows how we can live better lives—in doing so we help ourselves and others to become our best true selves. 2004 was a difficult year with the presidential election. Our minds were filled with world tribulations and the unrest in the Middle East. While we may not be able to solve the world's problems we can do our best to influence those around us in most positive ways. FM107.1 radio talk show host Ian Punnett has said many times on his show that "It's been said that we influence up to 250 people during our lifetime." Imagine how many more people we can influence each day when we live from our positive inner spirit.

There are no followers. We are all leaders and each of us is indispensable. We each represent a critical role or link. The chain is a connection among the finest people actively showing possibilities through "acts of kindness."

It is my hope that by the end of this book you will have already felt incredible improvement in your life. You will understand that "power" does not mean control. Your "real" power comes from living with integrity. This power comes from the deepest part of your spiritual energy…your soul. You will create the life you want to live with daily inspirations to bring out your intentions and support your values. You will know how to continually feed your body, mind, and soul in a positive way. You will become who you really are, and the "good" within you will naturally manifest. You will be living your chosen eulogy.

Soul Discovery

—Artwork by Artist Carol Dwyer Card

Trees…instinctively grow toward the sky. They also have long lives and the resilience to stand their ground, literally and figuratively, through all kinds of weather. Deep roots surely have something to do with it.

—Reynold Feldman, from his book,
Wisdom: Daily Reflections for a New Era

Chapter I

Soul Discovery

The man without a purpose is like a ship without a rudder—a waif, a nothing, a no man.

—Thomas Carlyle

Spirit is the essence and consciousness of one's soul—dark and enlightened. Both extremes are vital and should be left to flourish unrestricted. For in that journey discoveries are made.

—Film Actor Andy Garcia

Daily Inspirations

In order to live a quality life, you need to honor your spiritual well-being. In honoring your spiritual well-being, you need to find your calling. To find your calling, look and feel from within your soul. If you were living your eulogy, how would you want to be perceived? Living a "good" life is not the same task for everyone. Find a means that works best for you. I'm not going to ask you to keep a journal as many "self-help" books do because this is a "world-help" concept, letting your true self out to better our world. However, some of you may want to keep an in-depth journal throughout this book. Some may want a scratch pad to jot a grocery-type list of key thoughts and words. Or, you may want to break after each section to go into deep thought while sitting or going for a walk. Start out with **daily inspirations** to help you. At the end of this chapter, you'll find a list of daily inspirations, including a few from author Julia Cameron's book, *Transitions.*

3

In getting in touch with yourself, consider these questions:

- As you read, what interests you? What pulls you in and inspires you or motivates you?

- What were the most touching or meaningful times in your life?

- What seems to touch your heart in a movie?

- What's your favorite pastime or hobby? Is there something that you've always wanted to do but haven't?

- Is there someone you admire who is making great contributions to our world?

- When you're alone, what do you think about or what do you do…or what do you wish you could do?

- If your closest friends or family had to use one word to describe you, what would they say? Ask them.

- What are your strengths and weaknesses? What are your blessings? What would your "ideal self" be?

The Best Part of You

The point I'm trying to make is that the best part of you is what comes naturally…who you really are inside. Check out your natural abilities in terms of who you are rather than what you do. A role model can definitely help your process, but ultimately it's your unique take that will flourish. The above questions will help guide you to your true inner self and what your potential is. You may think of other more meaningful questions. They, in turn, may generate deeper ones. Go after the answers with all of your heart and soul, with your gut and intuition, and with utmost sincerity. "You must do the thing you think you cannot do," said Eleanor Roosevelt.

…the best part of you is what comes naturally…who you really are inside.

4

In her book *Angel Falls*, Kristin Hannah writes, "The measure of a person comes down to moments, spread out like dots of paint on the canvas of a life. Everything you were, everything you'll someday be, resides in the small, seemingly ordinary choices of everyday life. It starts early, this random procession of decisions. Should I try out for Little League? Should I study for this test? Should I wear this seat belt? Should I take this drink? Each decision seems as insignificant as a left turn on an unfamiliar road when you have no destination in mind. But the decisions accumulate until you realize one day that they've made you the person that you are."

I've attended many workshops where people are asked to write down their achievements. What I discovered was that most people write only those that were difficult to complete. But it's the achievements that come naturally and with ease that show what our true gifts are. Sometimes seeing the obvious is difficult. Asking questions of those who know you will help since they will state the obvious. Open yourself up to others and get rid of old patterns and beliefs. Beliefs are generalizations you make about what has to happen in your life to get the result you want. Your beliefs can keep you from experiencing the level of joy you deserve. You can change your core belief system by changing your perceptions. When you look at things from the outside in, you've opened your eyes to make clear your necessary path. "If you can imagine it, you can achieve it." If you're committed, there's a way to do it. Dedicate your life into uncovering who you really are so that you can truly give to the world by expressing your creativity and love.

Try to look at yourself as if you're watching a play, or movie or reading a book about a character. What do you like or dislike about your character? What changes would you like to make? Is your character gentle, patient, and honest? Or is it disrespectful, intolerant, and unfaithful? Be true to yourself in order to build a healthy foundation which can ultimately change your life. You

> You can interrupt your old patterns and habits and exchange them for what you truly value today.

5

can interrupt your old patterns and habits and exchange them for what you truly value today. This is what living the "good" life is about. It's releasing the bad energy to make room for the good energy to flow.

Advancing Yourself Advances Your Journey

Knowing yourself is the most important step in your journey. Before you can advance, you must be aware of who you are, where you are, and where you want to go. Once you realize which habits and beliefs are harmful and which values are powerful and real, then you can express yourself fully in your relations with yourself and others. "We can consciously become aware of the beliefs that drive us, the opportunities that surround us, and the effect of our behavior on others." (The Power of Flow, by Charlene Belitz and Meg Lundstrom.)

You can become aware of the effects your beliefs and behaviors have by starting a daily plan. Every morning before you get out of bed, ask yourself questions and visualize the day you have before you. Ask the questions as if it were a day you're creating. In order to change your beliefs, change your results ahead of time. Rehearse these results in your mind until they become so real that once you arise into your new day (real life), you'll automatically get the results you want. Don't think about your current place of work. One way to concentrate more clearly is by focusing on your breathing. Stop analyzing what's wrong with you. Focus on what you can do (are good at) for others. This is your day to give of yourself from your deepest inner self.

Here's an exercise from successful motivational speaker Anthony Robbins: Write down five of the greatest successes in your life that you didn't know how you were going to pull off, but you did. No matter what's going on, you can make it happen. Remember your five success stories whenever you encounter difficult transitions, the kind that make you doubt the good that is unfolding.

In creating your day while lying in your bed, ask this question: If you could do one kind act, what would it be? To help someone sign up for an ESL class? To be a listening ear? To accompany someone to the clinic? To be a library volunteer? To train as a hospice volunteer? Give of yourself physically or emotionally…anything…what would you want to do? What gives you goose bumps? Ask yourself what you want to accomplish today. What's close to your heart? What's your passion? If you don't use your enthusiasm and passion, you'll lose it. What has incredible meaning to you? It's not the same for everyone.

I have a tender spot in my heart for kids. Their early years are critical in their formation as bright productive teenagers and adults. I believe former Secretary of State Colin Powell when he says, "The youth are our future, and they are America's strength." I'm also drawn to helping kids with special needs such as autism. Throughout most of my life, I have given my time and patience to helping kids. I have a great appreciation for them, especially when I see their progress. I was not fortunate enough to have preschool or kindergarten, and I started first grade late. I learned from my peers in an orphanage. However, I was fortunate to be adopted into a very intelligent family that placed high importance on education. So, what would you enjoy doing for someone or some place? Tomorrow morning, begin with your questions. The poet Kabir writes, "Wherever you are is the entry point."

In order to live each day of your life with meaning and purpose, you have to do soul work. Everyone has a unique soul with a new lesson to learn in this lifetime. Gary Zukav, in his book *Seat of the Soul*, suggests that your soul may have gone through many more lifetimes than someone else's. Understanding your soul and the personality it has chosen helps you to understand the lessons it needs to learn in this lifetime. Once you can connect or align your personality with your soul, you can create great abundance in the universe.

> In order to live each day of your life with meaning and purpose, you have to do soul work.

That's when you'll be able to write down your eulogy and start living it. You'll have a deep sense of love and connection with a powerful Divine force. This spiritual hunger is created by you. Julia Cameron in her book *Transitions* explains, "Like a faint inner voice, it remains constant amid the stress of our busy lives. The voice of the soul calls to us and, although we may not hear it, it never stops trying to get our attention." Living consciously or in complete awareness will strengthen your ability to hear this inner voice. For some, connecting with their inner wisdom may be a gradual stirring, while for others it's a spiritual launch.

Life is too short to wait to see what may happen. Why not live the good life now? Once you live each day to its fullest by performing your greatest potential and letting your talents shine, you will feel incredible fulfillment and inner joy. Some make the connection through a religious context by placing trust in God, Tao, Buddha, a Higher Power; some may take a more nontraditional approach. Some choose to go on retreats, take meditation classes, pray, visit a sacred place, or become one with nature. Whatever your spiritual mission, the important thing is to live an authentic life that reflects who you really are...the goodness within.

Your Purpose

In searching for purpose, Charlene Belitz and Meg Lundstrom in *The Power of Flow* suggest "stepping out of our mundane pattern of existence into a larger picture. ...Turn your attention inward, compose yourself, and open your heart."

For positive lasting results in a demanding complex world, you need to find a daily spiritual practice within the context of your busy life. This is why it's so important to find who you are and what you are capable of doing so that you can create a lifetime of kind acts which come as second nature...or as "first nature" if you're connecting with your true inner self. It's a total life plan that's yours and no one else's. What works for you may not work for someone else. We are each a unique personality with a unique soul. Erich Fromm states, "Man...is always an individual, a unique entity, different from everybody else. He differs by his particular blending of character, temperament, talents, disposition, just as he differs at his fingertips. He can affirm his human potentialities only by realizing his individuality. The duty to be alive is the same as the duty to become oneself, to develop into the individual one potentially is."

We are all capable of creating a journey based on our own inner wisdom. Being in tune with your soul and living consciously is a lifetime journey. Your journey may contain benevolent and malevolent forces. We will make mistakes over and over, or we will listen to our inner wisdom and be aware the next time to take a different approach. Listen beneath the turbulence of daily life. Open yourself to the guidance of higher forces. Listen to the rhythm of your soul.

As long as we learn from our mistakes, we can create new positive energy. We must love ourselves first before we can love others. Once we can do this, we can continue the flow of goodness so that it may emanate through our personality onto others, therefore balancing our energy. When we become balanced, we become one with the universe. Our energy then, in turn, contributes to the balance of our universe.

You can preserve balance by maintaining a sense of calm and serenity. This is a goal attained through daily spiritual practice. Every day, make it a part of your life to feel, think, see, and act from the goodness of your inner true self. There will be both trials and triumphs, but each step is critical. In the end, whether a good or bad experience, that small step will set you on your path toward your true purpose in this world. Spiritual practice is central to your sense of well-being. Nothing should take precedence

> Every day, make it a part of your life to feel, think, see, and act from the goodness of your inner true self.

over your inner spirit unfolding. Take time and make the effort to touch base with yourself on a spiritual level every day. Make it a routine.

Conscious Living

It took me many years to see that living consciously means to have respect for myself and my life while pursuing what I deserve and what I truly want. But what did all this mean and how would I go about accomplishing it? What do I really want? What purpose do I have in this world? What are my values? I decided that in order for me to be the best I could possibly be, I would need a balanced life. I would later discover more about what this entailed.

Now I know living consciously means to fulfill your greatest potential by letting your true self emanate and radiate goodness from your heart, soul, and spirit in everything you do. It means you choose your thoughts, release negative emotions, and reinforce positive ones in order to live your highest quality life. Your actions do determine the effect that you will have upon others and the nature of the experiences of your life.

> Living consciously means to fulfill your greatest potential by letting your true self emanate and radiate goodness from your heart, soul, and spirit in everything you do.

After thoroughly examining my life, my values, hopes, and dreams, it crossed my mind to write my eulogy as I would want to be remembered, then live my life each day in a manner that would fulfill that eulogy. I realized that to live with this intention, I would have to work less, spend more time with family and friends, contribute to others and feed my mind, body, and soul. In starting a new healthier life, many questions arose. What would I look like if there were a hidden camera? How do I want to be perceived? What difference do I want to make in my lifetime? What would my eulogy be? Am I living "the good life?" Does the good beat the alternative?

Many of us react rather than act and lead. This book is about "acts of kindness" throughout your life. The good does win. Being nice means a lasting finish. When you emanate positive energy, the responses you receive from others are amazing. Even more powerful is seeing the domino effect. Imagine feeling completely fulfilled, filled with joy from giving to the universe and seeing it captured by others who continue the cycle of goodness. Imagine what a powerful world this can be if each of us lives daily the eulogy we have chosen.

Live consciously. Regular, repetitive, and soothing inspirations will become the stepping stones through your days. Daily rituals provide a gentle structure. As part of your intentional plan, watch and feel around you. What do you see in those around you that draws you to them or makes you feel good to be around them? They in turn will want to be around you.

A special friend of mine, Dan, who has been an independent medical consultant for many years, has brought great resolution to a number of operations with his incredible skill of not getting overwhelmed. He's able to creatively and diligently take something that needs a complete overhaul, form powerful individual teams, and create an entire new world, one that rises one hundred times beyond what the norm would have thought possible. As Morris Adler once said, "Our prayers are answered not when we are given what we ask, but when we are challenged to be what we can be."

My friend is a great example of going full force with all that he can be. He's in his mid-fifties, a time when many start thinking about their retirement years. But does that mean we suddenly stop living consciously? Living a simple, peaceful life does not mean that we stop contributing to the universe and stop being good to ourselves and others. Conversely, there are those who do not live consciously and don't think about their purpose on earth until they reach that magical age of fifty. Suddenly, you may feel that half of your life or more is gone and what do you have to show for it? Again, you hear that inner voice from your soul wondering what good you have done in your lifetime. What if you were to die tomorrow? Have you lived to your full potential? Have you tapped into your true self and wisdom? Don't wait until a magical age. Start now and continue to do kind acts throughout your life. Live what you would want your eulogy to be. Live today how you want to be remembered in the end.

Acts of Kindness

My best friend Debbie has natural genuine kindness. She's done kind acts for as long as I've known her...nearly half of my life. She's married with two boys and lives from paycheck to paycheck. She also has the daily pains of fibromyalgia. But that doesn't stop her. She gives completely from her heart—not only to her family but to anyone she meets. I am so amazed when I see how willing she is to take people into her home, to feed and care for them as if they were her own. Debbie and her supportive husband, Bart, do this while being financially strapped. I happen to be one of the many people Debbie has taken in. I lived with them for a year-and-a-half when I suddenly had to escape an abusive relationship. We are surrounded by many acts of kindness, which I'll talk about more in Chapter II, "There's an Angel in All of Us."

My friends Dan and Debbie are the same as you and me. They are traveling their journeys of daily events. The world is filled with people traveling "their" journeys. As you travel your journey, be aware of those who travel by your side. When you open your hearts to the adventures and adversities of others, your own journey is enlightened. Those surrounding you are your teachers and, in turn, you teach them. Appreciate the gifts of living life and see that all moments are valuable. At the end of each day, ask yourself of the people you had contact with: What value is this person bringing to me? What value are we to one another? Ask: What is the value in this occurrence? You can make note of this in your journal.

Our Changing World

Focusing on your values, daily inspirations, and routine are important, but also be completely aware of what's surrounding you. The world does change, and we must adapt our rituals to meet current needs, remembering that there is a higher plan in motion with which we can consciously cooperate. This acceptance gives us tranquility. Do not push your individual needs. Be patient, for there will be a proper time for its unfolding. Trust the universe and nature's timing. Do not push for artificial solutions. Remind yourself that your greater good often comes from adversity. Daily meditation and inspirations are significant, but we must not miss the many transformations before us that enrich our lives. View the good that works through all and in all, and embrace your destiny. Claim the good which it contains.

> Do not push for artificial solutions. Remind yourself that your greater good often comes from adversity.

Each of us is equally important in this universe. While we may offer something completely different, each of us has an incredible impact on the future. We are a part of the puzzle...the big picture...the very real world. We are each indispensable and add to the energy of the universe. As we evolve, so does the world in which we live. As we choose to act and interact, kindly and generously, our world becomes a kinder and more generous world.

Your True Self

Look in the mirror and look into your eyes. As someone once said "the eyes are the windows to your soul." What do you see? Where do you want to be in the great scheme of human events? Ask yourself today. Feel it and let it flow out of you. Once you take the first step, ask more discovery questions. If you had no fear, what would you want to accomplish? It becomes easier and easier every day because this acknowledgement is your true inner self coming out. It's an incredible feeling...better than any drug. You will automatically tune in to it more and more until you become the natural you.

We all have good souls and big hearts. It's just a matter of letting ourselves feel and be. All too often, fear holds us back. Often times, fear is manifested in our own minds. We think too much and wonder what the right thing is. The "right thing" comes from within. It's not forced. It's your true authentic self.

Have you ever felt like you do things based on what others want or on what you think others want? I did this for nearly thirty-five years. I always tried to prove myself, doing what others wanted at the expense of my own happiness. I did this for so long that I didn't even know who I was. I was constantly living for and through other people. I remember not long after I was adopted at about age seven, I was having dinner with my adoptive family. They asked me if I wanted peas or corn. I didn't know what to say because for so many years in the orphanage decisions were made for me. My identity was the culmination of a number of other people. I lived this way, shutting out my true self, for many years. And while I thought I was living consciously by proving myself and being the best I could be, I wasn't truly aware or in line with my soul. I was trying so hard to look good to others that I was living mechanically. I wanted to release and just be me but was afraid to for fear of what people would think of me. I am finally aware of how very special I am; my uniqueness is not ugly or weird. My true self is much more powerful and capable of making great contributions to the world than the "plastic me." Friedrich von Schiller writes, "Our own heart, and not others' opinions of us, forms our true honor." When you start thinking about what pleases you without holding back, it's amazing the person you'll see.

> Have you ever felt like you do things based on what others want or on what you think others want?

As you become clear in what you want, you become a channel for the universe to act upon you and through you. What an incredible inner glow you have, that's eager to dance and show what you are. Let out that angelic soul and let your creativity flow, with your own unique talents and skills. These skills are your purpose in this world. As Dory Previn said, "What most of us want is to be heard, to communicate." Let yourself be heard; communicate what you've always wanted to but were afraid to. When your communication is one of goodness and kind acts, not only will you receive positive responses but you will see the domino effect. What you transmit to others is then transmitted to more people. Eleanor H. Porter puts it like this: "The influence of a beautiful, helpful, hopeful character is contagious, and may revolutionize a whole town." You can change your life by changing your perceptions. It is important to appreciate yourself. Identify and cherish those character traits which are your strengths. Acknowledge and appreciate your accomplishments and talents.

Peel the Onion

As you move from the external edges of your outer body (armor) inward, you need to peel off the layers to get to the heart of your soul. By taking a look at each of your layers, you are taking responsibility for the conditions and circumstances in your life. You are the result of the life you've lived. However, you can leave the past and move into a future that is mapped by what is possible, rather than continuing on the path already walked because it is safe and comfortable. Oftentimes people find a feeling of security in familiarity and not knowledge. In order to have a profound understanding of the contribution you make to the world, you must get beyond the fear and get to your core self. As you peel the onion, you will experience your own commitment in ways that will inspire you and enhance your self-esteem, your personal effectiveness and your contribution to the lives of others. You will be the person you've always dreamed of being.

In becoming that person, we need to live with integrity, not judgment, and communicate with others. Don Miguel Ruiz in his book *The Four Agreements* explains it well when he writes: "1) Avoid using the word to speak against yourself or to gossip about others. Use the power of your word in the direction of truth and love. 2) Don't take anything personally: When you are immune to the opinions and actions of others, you won't be the victim of needless suffering. 3) Don't make assumptions: Communicate with others as clearly as you can to avoid misunderstandings, sadness, and drama. 4) Under any circumstance, simply do your best, and you will avoid self-judgment, self-abuse, and regret."

Creativity and Wellness

It is up to us to expound on daily inspirations, intentions, and affirmations and get a deeper soul connection to revitalize our creativity. You never know what the universe may put forth as a challenge or another learning experience. In order to stay true to yourself and continue to be authentic and good natured, you need to feed your body, mind, and soul. Mother Teresa said, "To keep a lamp burning, we have to keep putting oil in it."

What's fueling you? What gives you energy? Do your days consist of running on adrenalin, running on caffeine, running on fear, or simply running on empty? I've actually done all of the above at some point in my life. I've battled with insomnia for many years, so I know what it's like to run on empty...not getting enough sleep definitely affected my attitude and performance, as well as my ability to deal with people and function at my full potential. I've also run on adrenalin and have gotten burned out. Of course, the constant running—packing in the appointments and anxiety—did not result in high productivity. My "type A" personality was driving me to keep my schedule full, which resulted in a false sense of accomplishment.

After thirty-eight years, a diagnosis of avascular necrosis (a bone disorder) finally slowed me down to see that what I had accomplished was the breakdown of my own body. With all of the energy I exerted in hindering myself, I could have touched thousands of people and given of myself by simply being aware, conscious, and involved in my surroundings. I was in a whirlwind of constant giving, or so I thought, but with no true focus, authenticity, or sincerity behind it. I was doing for the sake of doing instead of being the best I could be by showing up; by opening my eyes to the universe and those around me; by sharing and letting others in. By giving from my heart.

Your attitude determines the quality of your interactions. Look at where your energy comes from. Are you putting your health at risk? What's important is not how long you live but how you live. Caffeine, anxiety, sleep deprivation, and fear can lead to long-term health risks.

> What's important is not how long you live but how you live.

Many of us run on fear. This kind of energy is negative, draining, and very stressful on the body and can affect our thinking. Even though I had earned a BA in journalism from Gustavus Adolphus College at age twenty-three, I chose to get married when I wasn't in love. I listened to others who convinced me that I'll never find the "perfect" man and that I should simply settle for what appeared to be a stable man with a decent job. My five-month marriage to an emotionally abusive alcoholic taught me that I should have followed my own gut rather than the voices of others.

I pursued my broadcast career, hitting the streets in high heels as a one-man-band, carrying a thirty-pound camera on my shoulder, tripod in hand, with lights and batteries strapped around my waist. When I became financially strapped, I went into furniture sales, making $50,000 my first year. The cutthroat atmosphere of a full-time sales position did not buy me happiness either.

Only you can make a conscious decision toward finding a healthy means of energy. Think about the things that make your body feel energized, your mind focused, and your attitude vibrant. Exercise, nutritious food, and a regular good night's sleep, are all examples of positive energy.

Also, just as important are the people with whom you surround yourself. Are they loving and supportive or do they drain you? Check your daily habits—really become attuned to them—journal about how each one makes you feel. Be totally honest. You're the only one that will see your journal. Which habits, hobbies, events in your life are positive and energizing? Which are not? Pick one negative, nonproductive habit a month to eliminate from your new life. Then write about how that decision is changing your life. How do you feel and act? You can choose to journal daily, weekly, or monthly—whatever works best for you.

Feed Your Body...

Take control of your physical body and use common sense about what works for you. If you have a medical condition that calls for certain exercise or eating regimen, then ask your doctor or a nutritionist what's best for your needs.

Breathing is also important and an extremely powerful tool. The key to a healthy system is deep breathing, along with muscular movements. This allows the blood to take the oxygen to the cells. Motivational speaker Anthony Robbins says, "Deep breathing exercises clean the toxins from your system and stimulate the cells. Take ten deep breaths three times a day, using the following ratio: inhale one, hold four, exhale two. So inhale to the count of seven, then; hold for twenty-eight counts and then exhale for fourteen counts."

When it comes to eating, many doctors and nutritionists suggest water-rich foods. They are imperative because eighty percent of our body is water. A large percentage of our diet should contain water. Fruits, vegetables, salads, and sprouts are all great sources of water. Every day, cells die and new ones form, so we need to cleanse and get rid of the wastes by diluting and eliminating them by drinking water or eating water-rich foods. Robbins recommends eating salads with every meal, and instead of dessert, eating fruit. There are many experts, viewpoints, and alternatives, but the basic rules are clear that we need more fruits, vegetables, whole grains, and less fat, red meat, and sugar. Everyone's body's needs are different, so ask a nutritionist about what vitamins, minerals, herbs, and amino acids your body may need.

Focus on your energy. Don't spread yourself too thin. This happened to be one of my bad habits. I had difficulty saying no; I, consequently, had too many projects with family, friends, and business. I could not focus and accomplish one hundred percent in any one area. My commitments put a lot of stress on me. When you overdo it, your immune system falters, and you're apt to get sick more often. Channel your energy and choose a couple things to do well.

In feeding your mind, body, and soul, remember to surround yourself with people that energize you. Find a partner who

In feeding your mind, body, and soul, remember to surround yourself with people that energize you.

supports you, who's on the same page as you in wanting to eat healthfully and exercise.

Feed Your Mind...

It's important to continue feeding your mind when you're in a relationship with someone. If you cannot have a stimulating conversation with your partner, then you may want to have a conversation with him or her about that. Be open and honest about your life desires and goals. Setting goals is a good exercise for your mind. It gets you thinking; your thoughts create intention which creates power. Your unique, individualized, creative talents will burst out into the world and not only change your life, but you will see dramatic changes all around you among other people's lives. This is the domino effect of your power. Learn to unleash your positive power within, and let it be captured by others who then continue the cycle of radiance...the genuine goodness.

The world becomes a much better place for everyone when we each release our power with no fear. Control your focus. Know what you want. Try something and notice whether it works or not. Then simply change your approach until you get what you want. If you become overwhelmed, let your higher power guide you. Manage your state of mind. Be very alert to your way of thinking and quickly replace any negative thoughts with positive ones. Mahatma Gandhi once said, "I will not let anyone walk through my mind with their dirty feet."

Another great way to keep your mind fueled is by creating your own collage. There are many self-help workshops that incorporate the idea of creating a collage of your aspirations, your vision of what you'd like to have in your life. Once you've thought about something, dreamed it, then put it in a collage (you may even want to hang it on a wall in your office or home). Then you can visualize and reflect daily on the direction you want to take in your life. Include your priorities. Cut out pictures and words from magazines which inspire you and glue them onto a piece of tag board any size. Mine is about five by four feet, and I consider it a "world-help" illustration. When you make your intentions clear, your desires will soon unfold before you.

> When you make your intentions clear, your desires will soon unfold before you.

Asking yourself questions is another mind fuel source. Remember what I said earlier with regard to your morning wake up routine? Asking yourself questions exercises your brain to create clarity in your intentions. Negative emotions may arise, which is normal, so feel them and let them penetrate you fully. Then replace them with positive thoughts. You may have your own ritual to help you think and feel positive. Mine is to do morning stretches while I ask myself questions about what I plan to accomplish for the day. After breakfast, I drink two cups of green tea while reading a book. I check my email and voicemail messages, prioritize them, and start my day. I do not read email or listen to messages before going to bed to make sure my mind is clear so I may have a peaceful night's sleep. I also find that I am able to handle any bad news on a message after I've done my exercises and eaten breakfast.

Breathing exercises, recommended by many professionals, is a key factor in attaining positive energy. Be careful not to let what you see, hear, and feel impact your health. Your mind can take information and run it through channels of fear and amplify matters to the point of self-destruction. It is up to you to be aware of your mental self-care and to be conscious of everything you see, hear, and feel.

Feed Your Soul...

Create real power. Align your thoughts, words and actions with the deepest part of who you are... your inner soul. This spiritual energy comes from living with integrity. If you had a day to do whatever you desire, what would that be? Would you read a good book, go on a trip, play a sport or instrument, take a class, change your career? We don't know how long our lifetimes will be, so be kind and generous to your soul. Nourish it by going to places you've always wanted to go. Spend time with loved ones. Create new hobbies.

We need to start thinking, talking, and behaving in ways that are congruent with our values and spiritual selves. Simply listen to your inner wisdom and live intently. Go with your intuition, that voice inside you, the angel within. By doing this, you are living your true values and beliefs, and this gives you ultimate power. This energy allows you to execute your greatest potential. You will not settle for anything less. When you do this, you are able to start each day fresh, inspired, and eager to implement your next act of kindness. This gives your life meaning and purpose...a life that you have created which honors your values. Acts of kindness will give you even more energy and power, creating great confidence and self-esteem, so that not only is your own life abundant, but you naturally exude that abundance onto others and the universe.

When you feed your body, mind, and soul, you're automatically attuned to your desires and are achieving what you prioritize in life. Once you've eliminated what drains your energy—whether it's a person, habit, event, object, or food—then you can live your "best" life. Trust yourself and surrender to a divine flow of energy, that will guide you to live that life. Once you feel this energy you will be amazed at how naturally everything progresses. Even if you cannot see the path ahead during those times of doubt, it's important to go back to the basics and practice the discipline of positive attitudes. It's your choice to get back on track and act in align-

> Once you've eliminated what drains your energy—whether it's a person, habit, event, object, or food—then you can live your "best" life.

ment with your true good. Have no fear to accept new opportunities, experience new adventures, and allow new acquaintances to enter your life. Choose to take positive risks rather than hanging on to the familiar, known life that did not allow for expansion and growth. Take that step out in faith despite your reservations.

I used to avoid making eye contact with strangers, or I'd turn my back to people. Outside of my home, school, and workplace, I would not go out of my way to approach others and openly communicate with them. I didn't socialize much and rarely had people over at my place. At school and work, I constantly kept busy so I wouldn't have to connect with people. I had very few close friends and many acquaintances. In school and work, I always got along with everyone and liked anyone no matter their age, race, or intelligence level. I, however, was not truly genuine; I had a façade, a mask I put on to appear friendly. I never got deep with people or let others get close to me. Imagine how you feel when you're in an elevator with a group of people. Well that's how I felt on a regular basis—from the grocery store to the break room at work to Christmas Eve at my own mother's house.

In most situations, my relationships and conversations were topical. For example, with fabric on your sofa, if you don't buy the additional Scotch Guard, which is actually sprayed all the way through the fabric, then all you get is a "topical" coating which doesn't last long. That's how my relationships were. Relationships never lasted long because I didn't allow the closeness. Another term for this is called a "commercial" application.

This reminds me of when I visited my grandfather in the nursing home for a few years. He was extremely intelligent, and even though he suffered from Alzheimer's, I learned an incredible amount from him. My grandpa, who was once so reserved, was much more open-minded and outspoken during his

Alzheimers. I remember one time when I was doing most of the talking (another way of not letting myself get close or intimate with someone), out of the blue, my grandpa said, "you're very commercial." He had a very unique way of communicating and sometimes struggled to find the right word, but as much as it hurt my feelings that he said that, it was so true. From then on, I tried to relax and lighten up—instead of always doing or saying something—I simply was being. I felt incredible warmth when I let myself be in touch with that moment in space with my grandpa. When I looked into his eyes and held his hand, it was genuine. It was an awesome feeling of energy I'd not felt before, and that energy was reciprocated as I could clearly see by my grandpa's eyes and smile.

A friend, Kris, someone I actually allowed myself to get very close with when I was eight years old, has a lot of fine qualities which I was fortunate to experience. After losing her for about twenty-seven years, we reconnected and I saw that same carefree energizing person. She was a lot like my sister Shannon; I've always wanted to be "carefree" like them—to be natural and real. I wanted to tear away the mask and the façade and let myself be open and free. Kris was one that would not only approach and talk with anyone in a grocery store, she would dance with them. Her amazing spirit is so full of joy you can feel it and almost see her soul dancing. Kris is a very good example of someone who has allowed her inner wisdom to direct her path. She is very much in touch with her higher power and feeds her soul every night by taking a walk with nature. She indulges in "visual soul food." She embraces trees and connects with the waves, sand, and rocks at the beach. She sings and moves with the wind. She lives her life every day based on "her" inner truth and her gut instinct of her true self.

If you listen to the wisdom of your soul and take action, you will find yourself headed in a direction that always leads to your highest good. Remember that it is critical to feed your body, mind, and soul regularly. Continually evaluate your life and listen to your inner wisdom by asking yourself whether your life events match your inner needs. It's important to take time to do this. Life presents many options, and you have control as to which path to take. Practicing extreme self-care will keep the connection to your true self open and available to you. Go with your gut inner instincts and your highest good will prevail. Have you ever had second thoughts about something, or has something just not felt right in your gut but you pushed it through anyway, then lost sleep over it, and eventually it blew up in your face? Think of all the energy used to push and pull before the crashing end result. This is why self-care is so important.

> Continually evaluate your life and listen to your inner wisdom by asking yourself whether your life events match your inner needs.

If your body and mind are healthy, then you will easily be able to make level-headed decisions to feed your soul. Don't be too cautious, however, and hold back on doing everything. Follow your instincts, and be very aware of what truly feels good. Trust your inner wisdom and act on it. Act and react with a sense of the larger view, your truer goals. Follow your dreams...your visions...your collage...your living chosen eulogy!

Evaluate Your Life

Now we will begin to create a life and influence others from a healthy standpoint. Use your new awareness to allow your wisdom to come through. You are in a position to make a difference in your personal, business, and recreational lives. Here's a short checklist to help you evaluate your life. Check each statement that you would say is true about you.

Lifestyle Evaluation

_____ I have disconnected emotions in my relationships.

_____ I need someone in whom I can confide.

_____ I need more intellectual stimulation.

_____ I need more alone time.

_____ I'd like more quality time with friends and family.

_____ I work in an unhealthy work environment.

_____ I work overtime when I don't want to.

_____ I take my work home.

_____ I wake up more than once during the night.

_____ I exercise fewer than three times per week.

_____ I eat junk food.

_____ I drink more than one caffeinated beverage per day.

_____ I'm engulfed by paperwork.

_____ My home is disorganized.

_____ I worry about my finances and making ends meet.

_____ I feel obligated to help others.

_____ I do something for myself fewer than two times a week.

_____ I don't have time for a vacation.

_____ I often feel unworthy.

_____ I drink more than one alcoholic beverage a day and/or smoke regularly.

The previous is a checklist of things that drain your positive energy. They take up a lot of time and keep you from living from your heart and soul. They mask what you want in life and what you desire to give in your life. It's difficult to find your purpose, live with good intentions, and have a meaningful life when you have a list of distractions.

Give yourself one point for each checkmark; then tally your score. Let's find out where your distractions or diversions are.

1–3: Good job. You are probably in touch with yourself and embrace most challenges. Now you can take action and follow your inner voice of wisdom to guide you through the challenges that still need attention.

4–7: You are beginning to live unconsciously and don't feel as connected with others and your true self. You know what you want and desire but something keeps stopping you.

8–11: You are overwhelmed with daily tasks and have emotional conflicts in most areas of your life. You consistently have extreme difficulty making rational decisions and find little joy in many areas of your life.

12 or more: You are in need of a complete overhaul. You are treading water and barely staying afloat. You are unable to connect with your inner wisdom due to your irrational state of mind, unnourished body, and unfulfilled soul. You're not sure what you want and feel you have no control over your thoughts and feelings.

In thinking about your relationships, environment (home), what you own, your health and well-being, your job, and your finances, ask what's working for you and what's not. Ask yourself if each thing contributes to your life in a positive or negative way. You are capable of moving away from distractions and into your inner core of who you really are and want to be. You have the power to tap into your wisdom and feel from your heart and soul, letting your true desires come alive.

We all have what it takes to find purpose and meaning. Yet you may ask yourself, what is the right way? How should I live my life? What do I have to offer? You each have a unique gift to share. That gift comes from within your unique self. The "right" way comes from your "true" self.

The "Right" Way Comes from Within

Everything you just read should help you to evolve from old negative patterns. It's never too late to do this, but the choice is yours and the right way comes from within you. As you evolve, so do those around you and so does the universe. The journey toward authentic power is the purpose of your being. As an individual, you are able to fully express your uniqueness and to connect with a larger whole. Knowing yourself at deeper levels allows you to go beyond yourself to connect meaningfully with others and the universe. Charlene Belitz and Meg Lundstrom in *The Power of Flow* say this connection with the universe is flow or synchronicity: "Synchronicity pushes us toward individualization by speaking to us in ways we uniquely understand, with layers of meaning and resonance that apply to our own lives and no one else's."

We each have the power and wisdom to bring forth our deepest values. This kind of power is one that does not judge people but has love for all and love for everything in life. When we become intimately engaged in our world, we experience authentic power. We have no fear and live life to its fullest every day with the utmost enthusiasm. We see all encounters as meaningful and do not allow ourselves to be destructive to ourselves, others, or the universe.

> When we become intimately engaged in our world, we experience authentic power.

To understand this realm, we must go beyond our five-senses to a larger perspective of the multisensory human as Gary Zukav, author of *Seat of the Soul,* writes. When we become multisensory, we are using our intuition and higher wisdom. Some may call this our "sixth sense." All of our great teachers such as Gandhi, Christ, Dalai Lama, and Mother Teresa are/were multisensory. Becoming multisensory is not a difficult task unless we make it difficult. We have created our own fears. We need to step back and peel the layers of that onion again until we reach our core greatness which is our soul.

We will be confronted with new challenges, and our fear will rise and we'll put up that wall, but the more quickly we can break through that wall and get through the layers of old patterns to our central good, the easier it will be each time. We can do this by not simply reacting, by taking a deep breath first and becoming very alert about what is happening.

You have the right way within you. How you respond to adversity is your choice, and your choices affect your evolutionary process. Zukav suggests that if you choose unconsciously, you evolve unconsciously. This is how our body or personality experiences and learns. The personality feels fear, anger, jealousy, and greed. But the personality is capable of love and compassion if it allows itself to connect with its soul. Love and compassion come from the soul's experiences. To be fully aware, and understand the influences of the soul, our personality has to become multisensory. This is going outside of the box of the five senses and recognizing that we have intuitions and gut feelings. This concept shows that multisensory people will look inside themselves while life unfolds before them. They learn to distinguish between the waves of emotional, psychological, and physical effects. They learn to choose to release the negativity and experience the positive energy from within. Over time, your personality can learn to identify with those effects and respond with love, thereby healing the soul and giving room to generate creativity. This is your individualized road to aligning your personality so that you can become who you really are.

> You have the right way within you. How you respond to adversity is your choice, and your choices affect your evolutionary process.

Each of us has an immortal soul that is full of compassion, clarity, and boundless love. The soul in each lifetime chooses to undertake new experiences in the form of a new body with a different personality to learn a lesson it yet requires for its healing. You need to love and to be loved. You need to express your creativity whether that's mentoring the youth or being a companion for the elderly. Becoming who you really are requires the understanding of your soul's needs. You need to cultivate your spirit. Listen to your inner voice and wisdom. What do you feel in your gut? Where is your heart guiding you? Let your mind bring it forth. Create from the inside out.

The questions we answered earlier should bring you to the next level of becoming what you've discovered about yourself—your desires and purpose. It's what the authentic you wants to achieve in this world, not what others or society bellows. You have the power, confidence, and courage to come out of your shell and experience and give from your deepest self. Zukav explains that by aligning your personality with your soul, you are in complete balance, in harmony, and you "cannot tell where the personality ends and the soul begins." Our bodies with our unique individual personalities are here as "Earth suits" so that our souls may function within the physical world. The attitudes we were born with serve the learning of our soul.

You have something to offer this world that's unique. No one else can give what you can give. You are a unique part of the whole universe. Expressing and sharing who you are consciously offers limitless opportunities for exploration and learning. Active discovery and engagement in the world creates growth and evolution for you and those around you. "The more aware you are of yourself, the more your expression will truly reflect who you are." (The Power of Flow)

> You have something to offer this world that's unique. No one else can give what you can give.

It is up to us to carry out our authentic good by performing the kind acts that extend from within our unique talents and skills. These "acts of kindness" meet the needs and wishes of the soul to live an angelic "good" life. Living through our soul is living our higher self—our fully awakened personality. This higher good and divine force is in all of us.

Here are two weeks of daily inspirations to help keep you on track, to help you live your chosen eulogy from your authentic good.

Collection of Daily Inspirations

From Kian Dwyer and Julia Cameron, author of *Transitions*

Day 1: I am blessed with abundance and I share my abundance with others. I am flexible and grow with the varied seasons. I see the wealth that each season has to offer to me and to others.

Day 2: I learn to expand my horizons. I look outside of the box as I search new depths. I am not fearful as I watch the present unfold before me.

Day 3: I find a quiet place to focus my attention on listening and feeling the inner stirrings of my heart and soul. I attune my spiritual hearing to deeper levels as I listen for the subtle signs which help guide me.

Day 4: I choose to accept myself rather than change myself. I will not hold in my natural wonders—gifts and talents—but will express them.

Day 5: I choose to be consciously aware of the lessons life is teaching. I consciously strive to see my options and choose wisely. I avoid falling into old patterns and behavior. I act with certainty yet with alertness.

Day 6: I am a student who can teach others by demonstrating compassion and giving from my heart. I speak kindly about myself and others, showing deep respect.

Day 7: I am aware of my progress. I recognize and encourage the evolution of me. I am a work in progress and celebrate my small gains.

Day 8: I embrace change and see the gift in adversity. I allow myself to move forward through difficult times by seeking the gifts (lessons) buried within them. I allow myself to experience and learn from new discoveries.

Day 9: "Today, I turn my attention to the lives of others. I open to the interactive dance of our intersecting lives. Alert and attentive, I learn from those around me. Empathic and involved, I teach what I have learned. Ours is a journey of shared hearts. I lift the lantern of camaraderie."—Julia Cameron

Day 10: "Today, I act with resilient optimism. I treat myself exactly as I wish to be treated. I am self-loving and self-respectful. I am the kind of person I myself respect and admire."—Julia Cameron

Day 11: "Today, I take a positive inventory of my assets. I count and consider my own virtues. I notice what I value, and I build upon those values. I become the person I choose to be."—Julia Cameron

Day 12: I release my fear and put faith in my higher power. I change what I can and accept the things I cannot. I trust that everything happens for a reason and choose to believe there's good in all.

Day 13: I express my vision. I show to myself and others my inner values, gifts, and desires. I listen to my heart and allow my higher power to guide me. I give time and attention to others in alignment with my vision and purpose. I know that my positive energy will create a positive chain reaction throughout the world.

Day 14: I enjoy the process of making my vision happen. I know that I am a work in progress and I feel fully alive!

Key Points

- Daily, ask questions to get in touch with yourself.

- Visualize what brings you joy and what is meaningful to you.

- Connect with your spirituality whether it's through a religious context or a more nontraditional approach.

- Be in tune to your heart and soul. Let your inner wisdom guide you. Learn from your challenges and mistakes.

- Feel, think, see, and act from the goodness of your inner true self.

- Be patient by not pushing for artificial solutions.

- Live by your values and not by what others think, say, or want.

- Peel the onion. Take responsibility for the conditions and circumstances in your life.

- Feed your body: Take control of your physical body, and use common sense about what works for your body.

- Feed your mind: Manage your state of mind. Be alert to your way of thinking, and quickly replace any negative thoughts with positive ones.

- Feed your soul: Living with integrity creates spiritual energy. Nourish your soul by going to places you've always wanted to go. Spend time with loved ones. Create new hobbies.

- Evaluate your life: Realize where you focus your energy and move away from those distractions. Move toward the inner core of who you really are and who you want to be.

- The "right" way comes from within your deepest values, which give you power and wisdom. This power does not judge others but has love for all and for everything in life.

- Become who you really are by expressing your creativity. Carry out your authentic good by performing the kind acts which extend from your unique talents and skills.

There's an Angel in All of Us

—Artwork by MaryAnn Millay

The angelic way lies within all of us. It's that euphoric feeling when we know in our gut we did the right thing. It's making a difference in our own spiritual way. We feel no weight on our shoulders and back, and no pain in our stomach and heart. We flow with ease, and the light of our heart and soul shines.

—Kian Dwyer

Chapter II

There's an Angel in All of Us

*I have never had a policy. I have simply tried to do
what seemed best each day, as each day came.*

—Unknown

*Your vision will become clear only when you can
look into your own heart.*

—Carl Jung

As we grow and learn, we are able to release the bad energy and emanate the angel in us. This is acting in alignment with our souls rather than with our personalities. We can create a reality that is of our soul versus our personality. To find our true callings or angelic sides we need to move our attention in a higher, more creative direction. This invokes the structures of a more enlightened worldview. When we connect and live from the angel within us, our hearts, souls, and minds rise and then so does the world around us.

When we have done the spiritual growing up, we realize that every human being is of equal importance. We have work to do in this world. We have equal potential, even though we may be at different stages of growth.

Oprah's Angel Network

In Chapter I, I asked you to think of someone you look up to who has made great contributions to the world. I, like many people look up to television talk show host Oprah Winfrey, who has put into practice the "acts of kindness" campaign through her Angel Network.

Through the Angel Network website, Oprah states, "I want you to open your hearts and see the world in a different way. You get from the world what you give to the world. I promise this will change your life for the better."

Oprah's Angel Network was established in 1997. Since then, she has collected over $3.5 million to fund college scholarships for one hundred fifty students in need. Contributions to her network include millions of viewers, celebrities, and advertising sponsors who have collectively raised over $12 million. Oprah's Angel Network has also funded over two hundred homes with Habitat for Humanity and has built thirty-four schools in ten countries.

Since 1986, I have watched Oprah's incredible spirit and tremendous desire to support and give to others and the world in any way she can. Oprah has inspired me immeasurably. Her show produces a beaming smile on my face. I also value the *O* magazine. Her spirit, heart, and soul and what she does for others is so joyful to watch, it gives me goose bumps.

For as long as I can remember, I have wanted to help others. When I was just twelve years old, my friends would call me Dr. Dwyer because I would listen to them and give advice for hours. Of course, my mother didn't care for the time I spent on the phone. As early as age ten, I thought I would grow up to become a psychologist. My BA degree consisted of a double major in speech/communications and a psychology minor. I continue to be fascinated with the operation of the human mind and behaviors. My education has helped me to mentor kids, including those with special needs.

I have also, for as long as I can remember, given materially. My favorite Oprah shows give away the house. It's one gift after another, and the audience screams in utter joy. I just smile and laugh and look at Oprah, thinking, "Wow, she's amazing. How I would love to give to so many people like that." It's wonderful to see the joy in people's faces. Even more meaningful are the Oprah shows wherein she gives the world to a family who didn't know when and where their next meal was coming from, or to the person born with severe medical challenges.

Like Oprah, I first pursued a broadcast career; unlike Oprah, I didn't make it too far. Not many positions make one financially stable in that field. You need to be an anchor at a large market station to make decent money. For a while, that didn't matter because I was so happy with reporting news that I didn't care about making money.

> Like Oprah, I first pursued a broadcast career; unlike Oprah, I didn't make it too far.

Unable to buy groceries for eight months and living on left-overs from family and friends, I finally decided to go into sales just to get my feet on the ground. Once I discovered the potential I had in making good money, I wanted to make even more. I started dreaming about paying off all of my debt and to being financially secure. I didn't want to have any car payments or a mortgage. I figured that once I was secure, I could help my family and friends. After that, I could really start making a difference in this world. If I won the lottery, I would not want a bigger house; rather, I'd want to help someone finance a new home or pay off their current one. John Wesley once said, "Make all you can, save all you can, give all you can."

Education is critical, especially the early years. I have volunteered and mentored kids since I was a teenager. We have the capability and responsibility to mold today's children by giving them love and courage, and teaching them values so that when they become adults, they can create a better society—a society that is caring and will bring out the angel in everyone. As Former President of South Africa, Nelson Mandela, says, "Without children, humankind ceases to exist." Helen Keller said, "It is not possible for civilization to flow backwards while there is youth in the world." It is imperative that we give every child the opportunity to have an education as early as possible. This is vital in developing their future human potential.

> It is imperative that we give every child the opportunity to have an education as early as possible.

I actively participate and contribute toward providing education for all youth. In the orphanage, I learned from my peers and spoke "broken Farsi," the Persian language. I was fortunate enough to be adopted into an intelligent family who had the patience to work with me. My mother sat with me for hours helping me with my homework. School came easily for my sister, but for me, success was due to my determination, perseverance, and an extremely patient mother.

I recently reconnected with a man named Greg who took me under his wing. We were once seven-year-olds together and only knew each other for a year and a half. I call him my angel because he was so compassionate. When I first came to the States, I lived in New Jersey. At age seven, Greg guided and mentored me with his young wisdom. He gave me hope. He was quite the brilliant not-so-small, seven-year-old boy. At age eight, I moved to Minnesota, but the hope he gave me stayed with me throughout my life—the hope to carry out my dreams and become the person I was meant to be. Greg is an incredible example of someone who lives from the angel within. He is of a good mold. This should not be a unique situation, however. It's important that we become angelic models and teach today's youth to stay in touch with their hearts and souls and to live compassionately. It is up to us today to mold the youth of tomorrow.

Oprah's Angel Network is an organization that provides that. The Network established the "Use Your Life Award" in 2000 wherein many people, including celebrities, have made a difference for others in need. One hundred percent of all donations go directly to the Angel Network organizations. Oprah communicates, "I would encourage you to look inside yourself, to see what you have to offer...and use that to give back to the world."

I continue to mentor youth. I have chosen to write this book in part to honor one of the most powerful women I've ever seen, Oprah Winfrey. She is one of the most vocal campaigners for children's rights and education. Over the years, she has donated $7 million to Morehouse College in Atlanta and in 1993 gave $1 million to a Chicago high school. She also handed over her $500,000 fee from the film *There Are No Children Here* to a local scholarship fund.

My other decision for writing this book is to start living my chosen eulogy by doing what I do best—informing, mentoring, and helping others. I am hoping that this book will create a "kindness chain" that will consist of an exponential number of people living their chosen eulogies. If we each live from our truest values, then our soul will create through our personalities miraculous achievements.

I used to look at Oprah and say, "Wow, she is amazing, I would love to be able to do that, I wish I could." Well, we all can make a substantial difference in our own way. Start writing a list of things about which you feel strongly or which inspire you. Write down what you see in others that ignites you. Connect your head with your heart, and you will be explosive. As Oprah says, "When you get, give; when you learn, teach!"

Oprah has a fabulous idea, and it works. The "kindness chain" is so simple and yet it gives you and your life more richness than you can possibly imagine. Your life will improve drastically, and you will feel better about yourself and the world in which you live. As I'm writing this on Thursday, July 10, 2003, I watch the clock as it nears 4:00 Central Time so that I can tune in to Oprah's show. I literally pause just before this sentence and turn on the TV to find that it's a rerun of Oprah's favorite things for spring. She generally gives away her favorite products to her entire audience at Christmas time, but for the first time this year she decided to have Christmas in the spring. I broke from writing to watch the rerun. Oprah said on that show, "My favorite thing is to make other people happy...so when I see something I like or it's a good product, I want to share it."

Connecting with Your Angelic Side

In connecting with your angelic side it's important to visualize first who you are. Sit quietly and breathe deeply with your eyes closed. You may want to put on some light music and burn candles. Whatever helps you to form an image of your soft, gentle dynamic, creative angel emerging into the world. Remember the true desires and talents you discovered in chapter one and see yourself creating a new life.

Once you've visualized it, then you can speak out loud with positive affirmations about yourself and what you plan to offer. Let your family, friends and people around you know your angelic mission. You may want to journal your ideas that you pictured during your visualization process and make a list of the affirmations (the positive statements) you spoke about yourself. This will help you stay committed to being who you really are. It's especially important in these initial days to surround yourself with positive people. This positive energy will accelerate your progress.

Connect with your feelings and find your passion, the angel within you and engage yourself with that spiritual gift. You may be very busy with your chaotic life, but it only takes a moment during a shower or bath to close your eyes and allow the emotion of your soul to emerge. What feelings come to you? Try this every day until your vision becomes clear and you're ready to make the first step. The first step can be to simply share your vision with someone close to you, someone who's supportive.

The next step will come naturally as you start noticing the way you act and interact with people. Every day life starts reflecting your soul's calling. You'll notice meaningful patterns and you'll find yourself deeply absorbed in a discovery that seems magical. You live for the moment being the best you can be by showing your angelic side to others.

You're contributing to the Universe simply by releasing the kindness of your soul. This release of your authentic self gives you incredible power. In no time, you'll be the leader of a new chain of kindness. You will collectively inspire others to follow the pattern and add another link to the chain. This is definitely not about the weakest link but the strongest best link. Only those with integrity and true sincerity and generosity will gravitate toward the "bring out the angel in you chain."

You'll notice meaningful patterns and you'll find yourself deeply absorbed in a discovery that seems magical.

Once you've tapped into your higher self and performed angelic kind acts, then you've recognized your meaning in life. Following your beliefs and values and displaying your rich attitude flows with ease, and others will be drawn to you like a magnet. They will feel your light passing through them to touch their most genuine soul, and then another link to the chain is born. That link is then the leader for the next and so on. So we are all leaders in this world and all have something special we can offer.

Oprah's Angel Network website has many ideas for starting a kindness chain, including a kindness journal to document your chain as it grows. You can write your name and address on the inside cover so that the journal is returned to you. Your journal will be a collection of good deeds throughout the community, state, country, and perhaps the world. After you write the good deed that you performed, then give it to someone else to do what comes from their heart and so on.

We all have souls that are capable of being loving and compassionate, but sometimes we are threatened and influenced by our society. This is when we become mean personalities. We need to step back and let our feelings penetrate through us, then step forward by thinking what end result we can create.

It's our choice and we have the control if we allow ourselves to feel, think, and then act responsibly, genuinely, and out of the kindness of our hearts. We all have the capability of letting out our inner angels rather than acting cruel. You can start out by doing things for your community, school, or work. You can perform a good deed for a friend, a random acquaintance, or a group of people.

The woman known as the Peace Pilgrim, whom I dedicate this book to, walked more than 25,000 miles on a personal pilgrimage for peace. In 1982, the year after Peace Pilgrim's death, five of her friends wrote the book, *Peace Pilgrim: Her Life and Work in Her Own Words*. A copy of this book was given to me by my friend Jan.

I had explained to Jan how at age thirty I had drawn up my will. I made lists of my personal belongings and who they would go to. Then I thought, instead of storing these treasures, why not give them away now and see them be a part of someone's enjoyment and use. A couple weeks later I received from Jan's shelf an incredible gift which is my new favorite book, *Peace Pilgrim: Her Life and Work in Her Own Words*.

The following is an excerpt from the *Steps Toward Inner Peace* booklet by Peace Pilgrim. *Steps* is not copyrighted. I found this material transforming and inspirational. For a free copy of the complete booklet or for more information visit *www.peacepilgrim.org*.

Steps Toward Inner Peace—by Peace Pilgrim

IN MY EARLY LIFE I made two very important discoveries. In the first place, I discovered that making money was easy. And in the second place, I discovered that making money and spending it foolishly was completely meaningless. I knew that this was not what I *was* here for, but at that time (this was many years ago), I didn't know exactly what I was here for. It was out of a very deep seeking for a meaningful way of life, and after having walked all one night through the woods, that I came to what I now know to be a very important psychological hump. I felt a complete willingness, without any reservations, to give my life, to dedicate my life to service. I tell you, it is a point of no return. After that, you can never go back to completely self-centered living.

And so I went into the second phase of my life. I began to live to *give* what I could, instead of *get* what I could, and I entered a new and wonderful world. My life began to become meaningful. I attained the great blessing of good health; I haven't had a cold or headache since. (Most illness is psychologically induced.) From that time on, I have known that my life-work would be work for peace; that it would cover the entire peace picture—peace among nations, peace among groups, peace among individuals, and the very, very important inner peace. However, there's a great deal of difference between being willing to give your life, and actually giving your life, and for me, 15 years of preparation and of inner seeking lay in between.

> I began to live to *give* what I could, instead of *get* what I could.

During this time I became acquainted with what Psychologists refer to as *Ego* and *Conscience*. I began to realize that it's as though we have two selves or two natures or two wills with two different viewpoints. Because the viewpoints were so different, I felt a struggle in my life at this period between the two selves with the two viewpoints. So there were hills and valleys—lots of hills and valleys. Then in the midst of the struggle there came a wonderful mountain-top experience, and for the first time I knew what inner peace was like. I felt a oneness—oneness with all my fellow human beings,

by Peace Pilgrim

oneness with all of creation. I have never felt really separate since. I could return again and again to this wonderful mountaintop, and then I could stay there for longer and longer periods of time, and just slip out occasionally. Then came a wonderful morning when I woke up and knew that I would never have to descend again into the valley. I knew that for me the struggle was over, that finally I had succeeded in giving my life, or finding inner peace. Again this is a point of no return. you can never go back into the struggle. The struggle is over now because you *will* do the right thing, and you don't need to be pushed into it.

However progress is not over. Great progress has taken place in this third phase of my life, but it's as though the central figure of the jigsaw puzzle of your life is complete and clear and unchanging, and around the edges other pieces keep fitting in. There is always a growing edge, but the progress is harmonious. There is a feeling of always being surrounded by all of the good things, like love and peace and joy. It seems like a protective surrounding, and there is an unshakeableness which takes you through any situation you may need to face.

The world may look at you and believe that you are facing great problems, but always there are the inner resources to easily overcome these problems. Nothing seems difficult. There is a calmness and a serenity and unhurriedness—no more striving or straining about anything. Life is full and life is good, but life is nevermore overcrowded. That's a very important thing I've learned. If your life is in harmony with your part in the Life Pattern, and if you are obedient to the laws which govern this universe, then your life is full and good but not overcrowded. If it is overcrowded, you are doing more than is right for you to do, more than is your job to do in the total scheme of things.

by Peace Pilgrim

Now there is a living to give instead of to get. As you concentrate on the giving, you discover that just as you cannot receive without giving, so neither can you give without receiving—even the most wonderful things like health and happiness and inner peace. There is a feeling of *endless energy*—it just never runs out; it seems to be as endless as air. You just seem to be plugged into the source of universal energy.

> There is a feeling of *endless energy*—it just never runs out; it seems to be as endless as air.

You are now in control of your life. You see, the ego is never in control. The ego is controlled by wishes for comfort and convenience on the part of the body, by demands of the mind, and by outbursts of the emotions. But the higher nature controls the body and the mind and the emotions. I can say to my body, "Lie down there on that cement floor and go to sleep," and it obeys. I can say to my mind, "Shut out everything else and concentrate on this job before you," and it's obedient. I can say to the emotions, "Be still, even in the face of this terrible situation," and they are still. It's a different way of living. The philosopher Thoreau wrote: "If a man does not keep pace with his companions, perhaps he hears a different drummer." And now *you* are following a different drummer—the higher nature instead of the lower.

IT WAS only at this time, in 1953, that I felt guided or called or motivated to begin my pilgrimage for peace in the world—a journey undertaken traditionally. The tradition of pilgrimage is a journey undertaken on foot and on faith, prayerfully and as an opportunity to contact people. I wear a lettered tunic in order to contact people. It says 'PEACE PILGRIM' on the front. I feel that's my name now—it emphasizes my mission instead of me. And on the back it says '25,000 MILES ON FOOT

by Peace Pilgrim

47

FOR PEACE.' The purpose of the tunic is merely to make contacts for me. Constantly as I walk along the highways and through the cities, people approach me and I have a chance to talk with them about peace.

I have walked 25,000 miles as a penniless pilgrim. I own only what I wear and what I carry in my small pockets. I belong to no organization. I have said that I will walk until given shelter and fast until given food, remaining a wanderer until mankind has learned the way of peace. And I can truthfully tell you that without ever asking for anything, I have been supplied with everything needed for my journey, which shows you how *good* people really are.

With me I carry always my peace message: *This is the way of peace: Overcome evil with good, falsehood with truth, and hatred with love.* There is nothing new about this message, except the practice of it. And the practice of it is required not only in the international situation but also in the personal situation. I believe that the situation in the world is a reflection of our own immaturity. If we were mature, harmonious people, war would be no problem whatever—it would be impossible.

> This is the way of peace: Overcome evil with good, falsehood with truth, and hatred with love.

All of us can work for peace. We can work right where we are, right within ourselves, because the more peace we have within our own lives, the more we can reflect into the outer situation. In fact, I believe that the wish to *survive* will push us into some kind of uneasy world peace which will then need to be supported by a great inner awakening if it is to endure. I believe we entered a new age when we discovered nuclear energy, and that this new age calls for a new renaissance to lift us to a higher level of understanding so that we will be able to cope with the problems of this new

by Peace Pilgrim

age. So, primarily my subject is peace within ourselves as a step toward peace in our world.

NOW, when I talk about the steps toward inner peace, I talk about them in a framework, but there's nothing arbitrary about the number of steps. They can be expanded; they can be contracted. This is just a way of talking about the subject, but this is important: the steps toward inner peace are not taken in any certain order. The *first step* for one may be the *last step* for another. So, just take whatever steps seem easiest for you, and as you take a few steps, it will become easier for you to take a few more. In this area we really can share. None of you may feel guided to walk a pilgrimage, and I'm not trying to inspire you to walk a pilgrimage, but in the field of finding harmony in our own lives, we can share. And I suspect that when you hear me give some of the steps toward inner peace, you will recognize them as steps that you also have taken.

In the first place I would like to mention some preparations that were required of me. The **first preparation** is a *right attitude toward life*. This means—stop being an escapist! Stop being a surface-liver who stays right in the froth of the surface. There are millions of these people, and they never find anything really worthwhile. Be willing to face life squarely and get down beneath the surface of life where the verities and realities are to be found. That's what we are doing here now.

There's the whole matter of having a meaningful attitude for the problems that life may set before you. If only you could see the whole picture, if only you knew the whole story, you would realize that no problem ever comes to you that does not have a purpose in your life, which cannot contribute to your inner growth. When you perceive this, you will recognize problems as opportunities

by Peace Pilgrim

in disguise. If you did not face problems you would just drift through life, and you would not gain inner growth. It is through solving problems in accordance with the highest light that we have that inner growth is attained. Now, collective problems must be solved by us collectively, and no one finds inner peace who avoids doing his or her share in the solving of collective problems, like world disarmament and world peace. So let us always think about these problems together, talk about them together, and collectively work toward their solutions.

> No problem ever comes to you that does not have a purpose in your life, which cannot contribute to your inner growth.

The **second preparation** has to do with *bringing our lives into harmony with the laws that govern this universe.* Created are not only the worlds and the beings but also the laws which govern them. Applying both in the physical realm and in the psychological realm, these laws govern human conduct. Insofar as we are able to understand and bring our lives into harmony with these laws, our lives will be in harmony. Insofar as we disobey these laws, we create difficulties for ourselves by our disobedience. We are our own worst enemies. If we are out of harmony through ignorance, we suffer somewhat; but if we know better and are still out of harmony, then we suffer a great deal. I recognize that these laws are well-known and well-believed, and therefore they just needed to be well-lived.

So I got busy on a very interesting project. This was *to live all the good things I believed in.* I did not confuse myself by trying to take them all at once, but rather, if I was doing something that I knew I should not be doing, I stopped doing it, and I always made a quick relinquishment. You see, that's the easy way. Tapering off is long

by Peace Pilgrim

and hard. And if I was not doing something that I knew I should be doing, I got busy on that. It took the living quite a while to catch up with the believing, but of course it can, and now if I believe something, I live it. Otherwise it would be perfectly meaningless. As I lived according to the highest light that I had, I discovered that other light was given, and that I opened myself to receiving more light as I lived the light I had.

> It took the living quite a while to catch up with the believing, but of course it can, and now if I believe something, I live it.

These laws are the same for all of us, and these are the things that we can study and talk about together. But there is also a **third preparation** that has to do with something which is unique for every human life because every one of us has a special place in the Life Pattern. If you do not yet know clearly where you fit, I suggest that you try seeking it in receptive silence. I used to walk amid the beauties of nature, just receptive and silent, and wonderful insights would come to me. You begin to do your part in the Life Pattern by doing all the good things you feel motivated toward, even though they are just little good things at first. You give these priority in your life over all the superficial things that customarily clutter human lives.

There are those who know and do not do. This is very sad. I remember one day as I walked along the highway a very nice car stopped and the man said to me, "How wonderful that you are following your calling!" I replied, "I certainly think that everyone should be doing what feels right to do." He then began telling me what he felt motivated toward, and it was a good thing that needed doing. I got quite enthusiastic about it and took for

by Peace Pilgrim

granted that he was doing it. I said, "That's wonderful! How are you getting on with it?" And he answered, "Oh, I'm not doing it. That kind of work doesn't *pay* anything." And I shall never forget how desperately unhappy that man was. But you see, in this materialistic age we have such a false criterion by which to measure success. We measure it in terms of dollars, in terms of material things. But happiness and inner peace do not lie in that direction. If you know but do not do, you are a very unhappy person indeed.

> If you know but do not do, you are a very unhappy person indeed.

There is also a **fourth preparation**, and it is the *simplification of life* to bring inner and outer well-being—psychological and material well-being—into harmony in your life. This was made very easy for me. Just after I dedicated my life to service, I felt that I could no longer accept *more* than I needed while others in the world have *less* than they need. This moved me to bring my life down to need-level. I thought it would be difficult. I thought it would entail a great many hardships, but I was quite wrong. Now that I own only what I wear and what I carry in my pockets, I don't feel deprived of anything. For me, what I want and what I need are exactly the same, and you couldn't give me anything I don't need.

I discovered this great truth: unnecessary possessions are just unnecessary burdens. Now I don't mean that all our needs are the same. Yours may be much greater than mine. For instance, if you have a family, you would need the stability of a family center for your children. But I do mean that anything beyond need—and need sometimes

> I discovered this great truth: unnecessary possessions are just unnecessary burdens.

includes things beyond the physical needs, too—tends to become burdensome.

There is a great freedom in simplicity of living, and after I began to feel this, I found a harmony in my life between inner and outer well-being. Now there's a great deal to be said about such harmony, not only for an individual life but also for the life of a society. It's because as a world we have gotten ourselves so far out of harmony, so way off on the material side, that when we discover something like nuclear energy, we are still capable of putting it into a bomb and using it to kill people. This is because our inner well-being lags behind our outer well-being. The valid research for the future is on the *inner* side, on the psychological side, so that we will be able to bring these two into balance, so we will know how to use well the outer well-being we already have.

THEN I discovered that there were some purifications required of me. The first one is such a simple thing: it is *purification of the body*. This has to do with your physical living habits. Do you eat sensibly, eating to live? I actually know people who live to eat. And do you know when to stop eating? That is a very important thing to know. Do you have sensible sleeping habits? I try to get to bed early and have plenty of hours of sleep. Do you get plenty of fresh air, sunshine, exercise and contact with nature? You'd think this might be the first area in which people would be willing to work, but from practical experience I've discovered it's often the last because it might mean getting rid of some of our bad habits, and there is nothing that we cling to more tenaciously.

The second purification I cannot stress too much is *purification of thought.* If you realized how powerful your thoughts are you would never think a negative thought. They can be a powerful influence for good when they're

by Peace Pilgrim

on the positive side, and they can and do make you physically ill when they're on the negative side.

I recall a man 65 years old when I knew him who manifested symptoms of what seemed a chronic physical illness. I talked with him and I realized that there was some bitterness in his life, although I could not find it at once. He got along well with his wife and his grown children, and he got along well in his community, but the bitterness was there just the same. I found that he was harboring bitterness against his long-dead father because his father had educated his brother and not him. As soon as he was able to relinquish this bitterness, the so-called chronic illness began to fade away, and soon it was gone.

If you're harboring the slightest bitterness toward anyone, or any unkind thoughts of any sort whatever, you must get rid of them quickly. They aren't hurting anyone but you. It is said that hate injures the hater, not the hated. It isn't enough just to do right things and say right things, you must also *think* right things before your life can come into harmony.

> If you're harboring the slightest bitterness toward anyone, or any unkind thoughts of any sort whatever, you must get rid of them quickly.

The third purification is *purification of desire*. What are the things you desire? Do you desire new clothing, or pleasures, or new household furnishings, or a new car? You can come to the point of oneness of desire just to know and do your part in the Life Pattern. When you think about it, is there anything else as really important to desire?

There is one more purification, and that is *purification of motive*. What is your motive for whatever you may be doing? If it is pure greed or self-seeking or the wish for self-glorification, I would say, "Don't do that thing." Don't do anything you would do with such a motive.

by Peace Pilgrim

But it isn't that easy because we tend to do things with very mixed motives, good and bad motives all mixed together. Here's a man in the business world: his motives may not be the highest, but mixed in with them are motives of caring for his family and perhaps doing some good in his community. Mixed motives!

Your motive, if you are to find inner peace, must be an outgoing motive—it must be service. It must be giving, not getting. I knew a man who was a good architect. It was obviously his right work, but he was doing it with the wrong motive. His motive was to make a lot of money and keep ahead of the Joneses. He worked himself into an illness, and it was shortly after, that I met him. I got him to do little things for service. I talked to him about the joy of service and I knew that after he had experienced this, he could never go back into really self-centered living. We corresponded a bit after that. On the third year of my pilgrimage route, I walked through his town and I hardly recognized him when I stopped in to see him. He was such a changed man! But he was still an architect. He was drawing a plan and he talked to me about it: "You see, I'm designing it this way to fit into their budget, and then I'll set it on their plot of ground to make it look nice." His motive was to be of service to the people that he drew plans for. He was a radiant and transformed person. His wife told me that his business had increased because people were now coming to him from miles around for home designs.

I've met a few people who had to change their jobs in order to change their lives, but I've met many more people who merely had to change their motive to service in order to change their lives.

by Peace Pilgrim

NOW, the last part. These are the relinquishments. Once you've made the first relinquishment, you have found inner peace because it's the *relinquishment of self-will*. You can work on this by refraining from doing any not-good thing you may be motivated toward, but you never suppress it! If you are motivated to do or say a mean thing, you can always think of a good thing. You deliberately turn around and use that *same energy* to do or say a good thing instead. It works!

The second relinquishment is *the relinquishment of the feeling of separateness*. We begin feeling very separate and judging everything as it relates to us, as though we were the center of the universe. Even after we know better intellectually, we still judge things that way. In reality, of course, we are all cells in the body of humanity. We are not separate from our fellow humans. The whole thing is a totality. It's only from that higher viewpoint that you can know what it is to love your neighbor as yourself. From that higher viewpoint there becomes just one realistic way to work, and that is for the good of the whole. As long as you work for your selfish little self, you're just one cell against all those other cells, and you're way out of harmony. But as soon as you begin working for the good of the whole, you find yourself in harmony with all of your fellow human beings. You see, it's the easy, harmonious way to live.

> But as soon as you begin working for the good of the whole, you find yourself in harmony with all of your fellow human beings.

Then there is the third relinquishment, and that is *the relinquishment of all attachments*. Material things must be put into their proper place. They are there for use. It's all right to use them; that's what they're there

by Peace Pilgrim

for. But when they've outlived their usefulness, be ready to relinquish them and perhaps pass them on to someone who does need them. Anything that you cannot relinquish when it has outlived its usefulness possesses you, and in this materialistic age a great many of us are possessed by our possessions. We are not free.

There's another kind of possessiveness. *You do not possess any other human being;* no matter how closely related that other may be. No husband owns his wife; no wife owns her husband; no parents own their children. When we think we possess people there's a tendency to run their lives for them, out of this develops an extremely disharmonious situation. Only when we realize that we do not possess them, that they must live in accordance with their own inner motivations, do we stop trying to run their lives for them, and then we discover that we are able to live in harmony with them.

Now the last: *the relinquishment of all negative feelings.* I want to mention just one negative feeling which the nicest people still experience, and that negative feeling is *worry.* Worry is not *concern* which would motivate you to do everything possible in a situation. Worry is a useless mulling over of things we cannot change. Let me mention just one technique. Seldom do you worry about the present moment; it's usually all right. If you worry, you agonize over the past which you should have forgotten long ago, or you're apprehensive over the future which hasn't even come yet. We tend to skim right over the present time. Since this is the only moment that one can live, if you don't live it you never really get around to living at all. If you do live this present moment, you tend not to worry. For me, every moment is a new opportunity to be of service.

by Peace Pilgrim

One last comment about negative feelings which helped me very much at one time and has helped others: No outward thing—nothing, nobody from without—can hurt me inside, psychologically. I recognized that I could only be hurt psychologically by my own wrong actions, which I have control over; by my own wrong reactions—they are tricky but I have control over them, too; or by my own inaction in some situations, like the present world situation, that needs actions from me. When I recognized all this, how free I felt! And I just stopped hurting myself. Now someone could do the meanest thing to me and I would feel deep compassion for this out-of-harmony person, this psychologically sick person who is capable of doing mean things. I certainly would not hurt myself by a wrong reaction of bitterness or anger. You have complete control over whether or not you will be hurt psychologically, and any time you want to, you can stop hurting yourself.

> Someone could do the meanest thing to me and I would feel deep compassion for this out-of-harmony person.

These are the steps toward inner peace that I wanted to share with you. There's nothing new about this. This is universal truth. I merely talked about these things in my own everyday words in terms of my own personal experience with them. The laws which govern this universe work for good as soon as we obey them, and anything contrary to these laws doesn't last long. It contains within itself the seeds of its own destruction. The good in every human life always makes it possible for us to obey these laws. We do have free will about all this, and therefore how soon we obey and thereby find harmony, both within ourselves and within our world, is up to us.

by Peace Pilgrim

Summary

Four Preparations

1. *Assume right attitude toward life.*

   Stop being an escapist or a surface-liver as these attitudes can only cause disharmony in your life. Face
   life squarely and get down below the froth on its
   surface to discover its verities and realities. Solve the
   problems that life sets before you, and you will find
   that solving them contributes to your inner growth.
   Helping to solve collective problems contributes
   also to your growth, and these problems should
   never be avoided.

2. *Live good beliefs.*

   The laws governing human conduct apply as rigidly
   as the law of gravity. Obedience to these laws pushes
   us toward harmony; disobedience pushes us toward
   inharmony. Since many of these laws are already
   common belief, you can begin by putting into practice all the good things you believe. No life can be in
   harmony unless belief and practice are in harmony.

3. *Find your place in the Life Pattern.*

   You have a part in the scheme of things. What that
   part is you can know only from within yourself. You
   can seek it in receptive silence. You can begin to live
   in accordance with it by doing all the good things
   you are motivated toward and giving these things
   priority in your life over all the superficial things
   that customarily occupy human lives.

4. *Simplify life to bring inner and outer well-being
   into harmony.*

   Unnecessary possessions are unnecessary burdens.
   Many lives are cluttered not only with unnecessary

by Peace Pilgrim

possessions but also with meaningless activities. Cluttered lives are out-of-harmony lives and require simplification. Wants and needs can become the same in a human life and, when this is accomplished, there will be a sense of harmony between inner and outer well-being. Such harmony is needful not only in the individual life but in the collective life too.

> Many lives are cluttered not only with unneces-sary possessions but also with meaningless activities.

Four Purifications

1. *Purification of the bodily temple.*

    Are you free from all bad habits? In your diet do you stress the vital foods—the fruits, whole grains, vegetables and nuts? Do you get to bed early and get enough sleep? Do you get plenty of fresh air, sunshine, exercise, and contact with nature? If you can answer "Yes" to all of these questions, you have gone a long way toward purification of the bodily temple.

2. *Purification of the thoughts.*

    It is not enough to do right things and say right things. You must also think right things. Positive thoughts can be powerful influences for good. Negative thoughts can make you physically ill. Be sure there is no unpeaceful situation between your-self and any other human being, for only when you have ceased to harbor unkind thoughts can you attain inner harmony.

3. *Purification of the desires.*

    Since you are here to get yourself into harmony with the laws that govern human conduct and with your

by Peace Pilgrim

part in the scheme of things, your desires should be focused in this direction.

4. *Purification of motives.*

Obviously your motive should never be greed or self-seeking, or the wish for self-glorification; you shouldn't even have the selfish motive of attaining inner peace for yourself. To be of service to your fellow humans must be your motive before your life can come into harmony.

Four Relinquishments

1. *Relinquishment of self-will.*

You have, or it's as though you have, *two selves:* the lower self that usually governs you selfishly, and the higher self which stands ready to use you gloriously. You must subordinate the lower self by refraining from doing the not-good things you are motivated toward—not suppressing them but transforming them so that the higher self can take over your life.

2. *Relinquishment of the feeling of separateness.*

All of us, all over the world, are cells in the body of humanity. You are not separate from your fellow humans, and you cannot find harmony for yourself alone. You can only find harmony when you realize the oneness of all and work for the good of all.

3. *Relinquishment of attachments.*

Only when you have relinquished all attachments can you be really free. Material things are here for use, and anything you cannot relinquish when it has outlived its usefulness possesses you. You can only live in harmony with your fellow humans if you have no feeling that you possess them, and therefore do not try to run their lives.

by Peace Pilgrim

4. *Relinquishment of all negative feelings.*

Work on relinquishing negative feelings. If you live in the present moment, which is really the only moment you have to live, you will be less apt to worry. If you realize that those who do mean things are psychologically ill, your feelings of anger will turn to feelings of pity. If you recognize that all of your inner hurts are caused by your own wrong actions or your own wrong reactions or your own wrong inaction, then you will stop hurting yourself.

> If you recognize that all of your inner hurts are caused by your own wrong actions or your own wrong reactions or your own wrong inaction, then you will stop hurting yourself.

Over the past twenty years the Friends of Peace Pilgrim non-profit organization has been devoted to spreading Peace Pilgrim's message. I received permission from the Friends of Peace Pilgrim organization to include in my book the following "Thoughts to Ponder" passages which are from *Peace Pilgrim: Her Life and Work in Her Own Words.*

Thoughts to Ponder

THERE IS NO GLIMPSE OF THE LIGHT without walking the path. You can't get it from anyone else, nor can you give it to anyone. Just take whatever steps seem easiest for you, and as you take a few steps it will be easier for you to take a few more.

———

When you know your part in the scheme of things, in the Divine Plan, there is never a feeling of inadequacy. You are always given the resources for any situation, any obstacle. There is no strain; there is always security.

by Peace Pilgrim

When you have constant communion with God, a constant receiving from within, there is never any doubt; you know your way. You become an instrument through which a job is done, therefore you have no feeling of self-achievement.

The spiritual life is the real life; all else is illusion and deception. Only those who are attached to God alone are truly free. Only those who live up to the highest light live in harmony. All who act upon their highest motivations become a power for good. It is not important that others be noticeably affected: results should never be sought or desired. Know that every right thing you do—every good word you say—every positive thought you think—has good effect.

Life is a mixture of successes and failures. May you be encouraged by the successes and strengthened by the failures. As long as you never lose faith in God, you will be victorious over any situation you may face.

When you look at things emotionally, you will not see them clearly; when you perceive things spiritually, you will understand.

Live in the present. Do the things that need to be done. Do all the good you can each day. The future will unfold.

There are many lessons to be learned and scales to be balanced. The laws of the universe cannot be altered for one's convenience. Humanity must learn to accept everything that life offers as a learning experience. It is for this reason spiritually immature people cannot be spoon-fed by someone else. The seeker must walk alone—with God.

by Peace Pilgrim

If you give your life as a prayer, you intensify the prayer beyond all measure.

_____

Although others may feel sorry for you, *never* feel sorry for yourself: it has a deadly effect on spiritual well-being. Recognize all problems, no matter how difficult, as opportunities for spiritual growth, and make the most of these opportunities.

_____

To attain inner peace you must actually give your life, not just your possessions. When you at last give your life—bringing into alignment your beliefs and the way you live—then, and only then, can you begin to find inner peace.

_____

For more information or to order a free copy of the *Steps Toward Inner Peace* booklet or *Peace Pilgrim* book visit *www.peacepilgrim.org*, *www.peacepilgrim.net*, or *www.peace pilgrim.com*.

CONTACT INFORMATION
Friends of Peace Pilgrim
7350 Dorado Canyon Rd., Somerset, CA 95684
Phone (530) 620-0333 – Fax (530) 620-7085

by Peace Pilgrim

In continuing to connect with your angelic side, be aware and conscious every day of your intuitions. Frances E. Vaughan in *Awakening Intuition* writes about four levels of intuition: physical, emotional, mental, and spiritual intuition.

Physical Intuition

Being in touch with your physical intuition allows you to recognize certain sensations such as a headache, stomachache, and other pains in your body which are telling you something. "Go with your gut feeling," is what one of my favorite managers used to say. He'd say, "Dwyer, if it doesn't feel right in your gut, don't do it." I have followed that adage for many years. It's amazing the stress we can create, even to the extent of its culminating in severe illness. When we're aware of our actions at every moment and make the best choice each time and we know in our "gut" that we did, then we are attentive to our intuitions and will have peace of mind and body.

Emotional Intuition

You can also tap into your emotional intuition by being aware of your moods. How do you feel each day with your family, loved ones, or co-workers? If you feel uncomfortable, that's a sign that something may not be quite right. Or something or someone may not be aligned with your core beliefs and values. Keep this in check by recognizing it, talking, or journaling about it. You may simply have some fears with which you've not yet dealt. Open communication rather than bottling it up will allow the angel to do the talking rather than the caged monster to do the blaring.

> How do you feel each day with your family, loved ones, or co-workers? If you feel uncomfortable, that's a sign that something may not be quite right.

We've looked at physical and emotional intuition in helping you to connect with your angelic side. Now let's think about your mental intuition.

Mental Intuition

You may find your mind wandering when you're driving; you start brainstorming while taking a shower; you may have had some very vivid dreams, which exercised your mind during sleep. I think, strategize, analyze, and do my best problem-solving when I first wake up in the morning. Whatever your form, take this information and organize it in your head. Be aware of the information flowing into your mind and "see" the answer.

Spiritual Intuition

Your spiritual intuition is the ultimate connection with who you are. It's your true authentic self, the core beliefs and values of your soul, and the light of the angel within you.

A special co-worker friend of mine, a breast cancer survivor, has expressed the light in her soul in such angelic ways. It's hard to believe someone can be so kind. Cindy does not speak unfavorably about anyone. "There's two sides to a story" is her daily motto, but she takes it one step further, suggesting that both sides have good intentions. She's able to find good in any situation, including her own battle with breast cancer. It has changed her life astoundingly. Before cancer, she was one that was able to see the good in others but not in herself. Being a breast cancer survivor forced her to connect with her true inner self and to see her capabilities, which increased her self-esteem. Whether she knows it or not, Cindy has handed down her gift of putting herself in other's shoes before judging and of seeing the good in everyone.

When we don't judge others and are open to whatever the universe brings, we are able to feel connected at a deep level with everyone and everything. Our lives become meaningful and purposeful and our struggles diminish while cooperation and ease becomes a way of life. When you live from the true good with that angel flowing out of you, then you are doing your part in this world. "Once you're in this state of receptivity, everything seems to support us in a way that enriches our life and helps us see our process and purpose more clearly," say Charlene Belitz and Meg Lundstrom in *The Power of Flow*.

> When we don't judge others and are open to whatever the universe brings, we are able to feel connected at a deep level with everyone and everything.

When you connect with your inner passion, you are able to give what inspires you. This passion is different for everyone. In preceding pages, you were able to go deep within to find your true self, your values. You then came to the realization that in order to grow you need to emanate your values throughout your life. Starting today, you can make a difference in this world with your talents, big or small. In the end, the results will be galvanic.

Surrounded by Acts of Kindness

My parents adopted me from a country where adoption was unheard of. They were in Iran for two years for business and decided they wanted to give a child who was less fortunate warmth and love. This was a big stretch in Iran, as my parents were the first of four test couples for the new adoption process. In 1971, they had hooked up with the American Embassy, who connected them with a young, lenient, liberal judge whose argument was that these kids were in the only orphanage in the country that was not disease-ridden, so they deserved to be put into a good healthy environment. Also, there was no proof of my religious background since they were concerned about placing a Muslim into a Christian family. I was not born in a hospital, and there were no records of my biological family since I was put in a basket at the doorstep of the orphanage. I am so grateful to be in America. Had I not been adopted, I would have been out on the street or married off at age twelve. I was one of only four Iranian children ever adopted by an American family from strife-ridden Iran. To this date (2005) adoption of Iranian children by American families is not allowed. I know how fortunate I am and am thankful for the life this adoption has afforded me.

> I was one of only four Iranian children ever adopted by an American family from strife-ridden Iran.

We are all surrounded by kind acts. Sometimes in the hustle and bustle of our daily lives, we are not aware of or we take for granted the good that envelopes

> All too often, we focus on the negative acts around us and use up our energy in trying to fight a no-win battle.

us. All too often, we focus on the negative acts around us and use up our energy in trying to fight a no-win battle.

Start taking note of everything in your environment. When you stop at the gas station to fill up your tank and get a cup of coffee, be aware of the guy who moves his car up so you have better access to your pump. When you go in to pay, notice the smile on the clerk's face as she asks if you would like a cover for your coffee. When you stop at the bank, take note of the friendly "Hello, how are you today?" When you go to work and your desk has piles of problems, take a deep breath and remember the feeling you got from the warm smiles, voices, and expressions earlier in the day. You know that if you let those problems get to you, they will change your tone and mood. Focus on your voice, put a smile on your face, then pick up the phone and make your first call. Your tone and attitude will affect the end result of your conversation. You determine the outcome of your days. Learn not to take the good around you for granted. Let it energize you. You will then emit that onto others, who automatically transmit that radiance into their environment and so on. You will have turned a "hellacious" day into a productive one that leaves you feeling serene.

I'm amazed at the great number of kind acts performed around me, and yet we need to reach the many more people in this world to help them fulfill their natural acts of kindness in order to make those numbers increase.

I have been fortunate to experience my friend Debbie's kind acts. She has given so much with very limited finances and has touched a lot of people. Yet she tells me that she doesn't get this "soul searching" stuff. Her heart and soul exudes love every day in how she interacts with others. She is extremely compassionate and shows this daily. She cries at movies because she feels so much for the person who's troubled. She's an animal lover with three dogs and cats, fish, rats, ducks, and an iguana. She takes in dogs and cats who suffer from blindness, cerebral palsy, and other handicaps. She thinks of herself as a simple mother with two boys and a husband, who each day struggles to make ends meet. I see her as someone who's always there for everyone. She has had many friends—single, married, or divorced—with different life challenges, for whom she immediately opens up her heart and sometimes her home. I was one of the many people she took in and fed and provided for with no expectation of anything in return. She would tease me about the types of books I was drawn to on spiritual healing and living, yet she is an amazing healer and lover of all people. She's the most nondiscriminatory person I know. To love and to care comes so naturally for her that she doesn't realize it's a gift that some people search to find and experience. Sometimes the obvious is hard to see.

To help find the angel in you, ask your family and closest friends what they like most about you. They may say you're great with kids. Or you may be a good listener and companion. You could be a good storyteller with the elderly. Maybe you have a great love for animals. Maybe you're very domestic and like to clean or cook. Many of these talents that come to you naturally are what you can expand on and give to the world. These are your angelic ways and the reason why you're here. Everybody has a different gift. By asking your friends and family, you will be able to better connect with who you really are. You'll be able to do what you feel strongly about without fear. Sometimes you just need to hear it from someone else to realize, "Wow, yes, this is what I'm good at and enjoy doing." Find your passion, and use it to give what most inspires you.

> To help find the angel in you, ask your family and closest friends what they like most about you.

Kindness seems to run in Debbie's entire family. Her cousin Greg, who's in his forties, never married. Highly intelligent, he is in the electronics business and has an incredible knack for computers. He may not realize it, but his gift is just that. He has the time to share his intelligence, spending many hours setting up computers and teaching the use of them. He has also been generous with his hard-earned money. He has given away computers and helped others with the financing of their homes, cars, and other projects. He has performed many kind acts by giving of his time, service, and money. You can do this, too. Make a difference in this world by reaching out to more people.

In January 2003, I was diagnosed with avascular necrosis, a bone disorder wherein the blood does not flow through the bones so the bones disintegrate. There is no cure. I was told I would need surgery on both feet, both knees, and possibly both hips and that this could spontaneously affect other bones with no guarantee of the end results of the surgeries. The surgeries began with the right foot and knee so that my driving leg could have a head start.

MaryAnn, my friend's mother, was there for me during my emotional roller coaster ride after my medical diagnosis. I talked to her every other day, giving her updates on my condition, the test results, and my emotional state. I have her to thank for my part-time job as a teacher's assistant at a preschool. I had no teaching experience other than volunteer mentoring, but she had faith in me and was able to further my passion to be a part of creating a positive learning environment for children.

I always said that I would not want to be a burden on anyone, yet the caretaker in me was always willing to help others. However, to receive love and help was difficult for me. After my right leg surgeries, I couldn't drive for over two months; others had to drive, buy my groceries, and help me around the house with everyday needs. What amazed me through this experience was the number of people who came out of nowhere to help me. It was incredible. I allowed myself to receive the generosity and love of others, which helped me embrace the change.

> I always said that I would not want to be a burden on anyone, yet the caretaker in me was always willing to help others.

The parents of the preschool kids called, offering to give me rides to and from school, sometimes more than an hour each way with rush hour traffic. They felt I had something to offer their kids and that I could teach them even with my leg elevated. The director of the school, Stephanie, also looked out for me. The school continued to pay me even while I was recovering at my mom's house. Her surprising act of kindness helped alleviate my financial burden.

There are so many acts of kindness surrounding us. I've named some people in my life that have illuminated the angel within. Take a look around you, and be aware and conscious of your everyday life and existence. Be in touch with your surroundings, and you will experience many kind acts. When you see the angels around you, you will want to let out the angel within you. If you believe your higher self is your guide and loving teacher, then that will manifest.

Celebrity Angelic Acts

I've already talked about my idol, Oprah Winfrey, but there are many other celebrities who have radiated their angelic sides. Sometimes seeing people in the limelight blinds us from the fact that these celebrities make great contributions in enhancing, improving, and developing the world in which we live. CNN founder Ted Turner donated $1 billion to the United Nations and said, "I'm not going to rest until all of the world's problems have been solved." Actor Keanu Reeves, a committed Buddhist, is renowned for his minimalist lifestyle and amazingly big heart. Of his $70 million earnings from the *Matrix* sequels, Reeves gave $50 million to the costume and special effects team and took only $20 million for himself. Reeves, who has a sister with leukemia has also given generously toward cancer research. The world's richest man, Bill Gates, is also its biggest philanthropist.

In 1999, he pledged $1 billion to college scholarships for minority students. It was the largest-ever education donation. He has vowed that he will give away ninety-five percent of his worth during his lifetime. By 2002, valued at $43 billion, he had already channeled over $25 billion into the Bill and Melinda Gates Foundation, which fights AIDS and provides medicine and education to the world's disadvantaged.

Ted Turner, Keanu Reeves, and Bill Gates are just a few of the many celebrities who have donated insurmountable amounts of money to those less fortunate. Celebrity donations to organizations range from churches, schools, crippled children's foundations, the American Cancer Society, organ transplant locations, animal shelters, educational and medical programs for underdeveloped countries, disaster relief and food aid programs, adoption agencies, and awareness programs for diseases including diabetes, AIDS, multiple sclerosis, muscular dystrophy, Parkinson's, etc. These people have donated anywhere from $10,000 to a half million dollars annually, biannually, and sometimes quarterly to such organizations.

Ted Turner, Keanu Reeves, and Bill Gates are just a few of the many celebrities who have donated insurmountable amounts of money to those less fortunate.

The above information comes from the Washington-based *Chronicle of Philanthropy* published each year in February (2002–2003). *Chronicle of Philanthropy* editor Stacy Palmer told the *Observer* that the number of Hollywood names is scarce. She and television billionaire Haim Saban have expressed their feelings on the "stinginess" of many Hollywood celebrities. However, society is heading in the right direction each year with the percentage of celebrity giving increasing. There has been an even larger increase among large companies such as Wal-Mart and Target. The *Chronicle of Philanthropy* lists the top company (business owners) and celebrity contributions.

Most of us do not make the kind of money these celebrities make, but one small gift, donation, or act of kindness can go just as far and have the same powerful impact. The reason is that one kind act is usually followed by another kind act and another. When you do your best, others around cannot help but do the same. This positive chain reaction is what can change our world. Start the chain. If you should run into a challenging obstacle, remember the angel within will continue to radiate. Don't let difficulties sink you. Simply do the best you can every day and keep climbing the vertical path.

Quotes from World-Changing Leaders

It often requires more courage to dare to do right than to fear to do wrong.

—Abraham Lincoln

If you haven't any charity in your heart, you have the worst kind of heart trouble.

—Bob Hope

When you cease to make a contribution, you begin to die.

—Eleanor Roosevelt

When we accept tough jobs as a challenge and wade into them with joy and enthusiasm, miracles can happen.

—Gilbert Arland

The primary cause of unhappiness in the world today is…lack of faith.

—Carl Jung

Pity the human being who is not able to connect faith within himself with the infinite…He who has faith has…an infinite reservoir of courage, hope, confidence, calmness, and assuring trust that all will come out well—even though to the world it may appear to come out most badly.

—B.C. Forbes

The future belongs to people who see possibilities before they become obvious.

—Ted Levitt

Aim at the sun, and you may not reach it; but your arrow will fly far higher than if aimed at an object on a level with yourself.

—Joel Hawes

Do all the good you can, in all the ways you can, to all the souls you can, in every place you can, at all the times you can, with all the zeal you can, as long as ever you can.

—John Wesley

He that does good to another does good also to himself, not only in the consequence, but in the very act. For the consciousness of well-doing is in itself ample reward.

—Seneca

Undertake something that is difficult; it will do you good. Unless you try to do something beyond what you have already mastered, you will never grow.

—Ronald E. Osborn

If we don't change, we don't grow. If we don't grow, we are not really living. Growth demands a temporary surrender of security.

—Gail Sheehy

We are what we repeatedly do. Excellence, then, is not an act, but a habit.

—Aristotle

We're not primarily put on this Earth to see through one another, but to see one another through.

—Peter De Vries

The human spirit is stronger than anything that can happen to it.

—George C. Scott

A kind heart is a fountain of gladness, making everything in its vicinity freshen into smiles.

—Washington Irving

Human kindness has never weakened the stamina or softened the fiber of a free people. A nation does not have to be cruel in order to be tough.

—Franklin D. Roosevelt

Kindness in words creates confidence; kindness in thinking creates profoundness; kindness in giving creates love.

—Lao-Tzu

Kind words can be short and easy to speak, but their echoes are truly endless.

—Mother Teresa

In any moment of decision, the best thing you can do is the right thing, the next best thing is the wrong thing, and the worst thing you can do is nothing.

—W.S. Gilbert

We are all faced with a series of great opportunities brilliantly disguised as impossible situations.

—Chuck Swindoll

If there is hope in the future, there is power in the present.

—John Maxwell

Only those who will risk going too far can possibly find out how far one can go.

—T.S. Eliot

If you play it safe in life, you've decided that you don't want to grow anymore.

—Shirley Hufstedler

I know in my heart that man is good. That what is right will always eventually triumph. And there's purpose and worth to each and every life.

—Ronald Reagan

Key Points

- Move your attention in a higher direction by creating a reality that's of your soul and angelic side.

- Make a difference by seeing what you have to offer and give that to the world.

- Visualize your angelic mission, using positive affirmations, and let your family, friends, and other people know your mission.

- Your life will naturally reflect your soul's calling where you'll notice significant, meaningful patterns.

- Choose your thoughts and feelings, act responsibly and from the kindness of your heart in your daily life in everything you do.

- Be in touch with your physical, emotional, mental, and spiritual intuitions.

- Be aware of the good that surrounds you rather than taking kind acts for granted.

- You have a talent to contribute, which will enhance, improve, and develop the world you live in.

Kill Them with Kindness

—Artwork by Artist Carol Dwyer Card

Our true gift is knowing how to manage our doubt, fear, and anger. Even when adversity or abrasive words and actions strike, we choose not to bite back but to kill with kindness.

—Kian Dwyer

Chapter III

Kill Them with Kindness

*Constant kindness can accomplish much. As the
sun makes ice melt, kindness causes misunder-
standing, mistrust, and hostility to evaporate.*

—**Albert Schweitzer**

*The beauty of the soul shines out when a man bears
with composure one heavy mischance after another,
not because he does not feel them, but because he is
a man of high and heroic temper.*

—**Aristotle**

When we continue to live from our goodness within, we will make a vast difference in our everyday lives among all those with whom we come into contact. We can choose to stay on the horizontal path of what's familiar and not grow, or we can live to our full potential. When we give kindness from the goodness of our heart with no selfish motive, we'll move up the path in abundance and joy. This vertical path is unstoppable even when we run into adversity or a vile person. You will learn to follow your heart and trust your intuition. Remember the physical, emotional, mental, and spiritual intuitions from Chapter II.

Follow your intuition and inner voice of wisdom when you're confronted with a bad situation. Detach yourself and look at it objectively. When you do this, you are not taking it personally. Instead of dwelling on the negative, immerse yourself in positive energy. You may have let a situation bother you for weeks, months, and even years. The result is a disconnection from your inner beliefs and values. This disconnection creates pain in your heart and affects your mind and body to the point of creating scattered thoughts and actions. This may result in a headache or stomachache. You may have held grudges, and acted out unfavorably. Increase your awareness simply by being in tune to how you think and feel when something like this occurs. Catch yourself before acting out in spite.

Now you know how to connect with your heart and soul to better understand your true self. You can control your emotions by stepping back, taking a deep breath and visualizing the angel within. It's up to you to change old patterns, to break from your reality of life as you have been living it. Rather than letting malicious acts by others torment you, you can kill them with kindness. Instead of doling out your kindness to those who deserve it and reprimanding those who don't, remember that showing your love and living from the goodness of your heart wins the day.

However, as Peace Pilgrim in the book *Peace Pilgrim* says, it's not healthy to bottle up your feelings. "Do not suppress your feelings—that would hurt you inside. Do not express it—this would not only hurt you inside, it would cause ripples in your surroundings. What you do is transform it. You somehow use that tremendous energy constructively on a task that needs to be done, or in a beneficial form of exercise."

Transforming ourselves from bad habits puts us in touch with our true selves. Getting in touch with your essence and allowing others to do the same takes strength and perseverance. To construct new values, beliefs, understanding, and reality, we need to explore and know there are always possibilities.

Explore Possibilities

There are people who make things happen, those who watch what happens, and those who wonder what happened.

—Unknown

We all add a spiritual value to the world. To remain a spiritual person who performs humanitarian acts, you'll need to be brave, as

Cheryl Richardson writes in her book, *Life Makeovers:* "You'll need courage and strength of character that will allow you to step off the common path and stand up to ridicule, criticism, and the inevitable fear, insecurity, and self-questioning that will occur." Be careful, though, to be true to yourself and live with integrity.

In Chapter I, you uncovered your inner beliefs, morals, and values. I learned the hard way that I sometimes cared more about being liked than about following my heart and my values. I have since learned to surround myself with people who share similar values. In Chapter II, you discovered more fully the angel within you and in others. In this chapter, you'll learn how to continue being who you are and act in kindness even when misfortunes strike.

If you seem to be having a bad day or week wherein everything seems to be a struggle, take note of your actions and thoughts preceding those negative events. You control your thoughts and actions, and when you get into a rut, you are the only one that can make the responsible choices to get yourself back out. Remember that when you radiate positive energy, others cannot help but to continue that positive cycle. By being the best you can be, you, in turn, encourage others to be the best that they can be. Your actions need to be truthful and genuine though.

> If you seem to be having a bad day or week wherein everything seems to be a struggle, take note of your actions and thoughts preceding those negative events.

Darla, a public relations executive in her forties, felt exhausted and depressed. She felt as though she was always doing favors for people at work, for her husband and kids at home, and for friends and family, yet things seemed to always go wrong for her. She struggled with her relationships at home and work. People were always coming to her with their problems, and it was draining. She felt she was constantly being kind to others and yet felt no one treated her well. She was beginning to feel unworthy. As her spiritual mentor, I asked her a few questions. She couldn't come up with any answers that proved her unworthiness. But she did come to the realization that she helped others in hopes of getting something in return and that she reacted negatively when others were not kind to her.

In exploring the possibilities, we came up with a new plan. Darla would only give when her generosity was genuine and without expectations. When she did act kindly toward someone and they continued to treat her unfavorably, she would not react. Sometimes, whether it's at work or home, it's important to distance yourself. Get up and go outside or take a brief break. After a few months, Darla noticed a considerable difference in the way she felt and how others were treating her.

It's important to point out, as with Darla's situation, that you don't go overboard in helping others. This may be your purpose in life but it needs to be healthy and energizing. While helping others fulfills your soul, it can also be detrimental if it results in neglecting your own life. When you go too far and spread yourself too thin, this drains your energy and doesn't feed your soul. Remember the importance of self-care discussed in Chapter I; continue to be aware of your needs. Watch your fuel resources: the healthy things that feed your body, mind, and soul.

Think of all events as a learning experience to help in your growth and to create possibilities in bettering your life and the world. You may have thought in the past that a particular event was a tragedy, terrible, awful, or bad. "Why did it happen to me?" You can change your way of thinking by being intuitive to your feelings and thoughts, thereby allowing only the goodness of your heart and soul to come out. Difficulties are opportunities for inner growth. The greater the difficulty the greater the opportunity for growth. Adversity is a "gift," part of life's learning process and the evolution of you. With each situation every day at home, work, or at play, it is up to you to create positive energy and to live from your soul.

Your values come from your soul. In order to keep living and meeting the needs of your soul, you must balance your energy. To paraphrase Zukav, if one takes advantage of another then that throws off their energy. In order to balance that energy, the one who took advantage of another will in turn be taken advantage of by others. There's a lesson to be learned here. Explore this, and be very conscious and aware of your everyday actions.

Connecting with our inner wisdom does not mean that we are superior to others. We are not to be judgmental of others. When we lose a loved one or a relationship ends or we're involved in a car accident or we see terrorist threats and bombings in our world or we end up with a terminal illness, we are to learn from these misfortunes.

Connecting with our inner wisdom does not mean that we are superior to others.

Someone once said, "There is a piece of fortune in misfortune." Even the greatest most painful misfortune, in the end, can bring us much happiness.

On September 11, 2001, America and the world were in shock when terrorist attacks occurred on four United States airline flights. Two of the planes crashed into the World Trade Center towers, one crashed into the Pentagon and another into the ground in Pennsylvania. Several thousand people died and our nation is slowly recovering from the shock of this tragedy. Lisa Beamer, wife of Todd Beamer who was on flight 93 (which crashed in Pennsylvania) wrote a book titled *Let's Roll,* Todd's last words. Todd lived his life well until the very end. Throughout his life, he performed many acts of kindness, especially in his church by mentoring the youth on spirituality. Lisa has taken the 9-11 tragedy and turned it into a gift by touching millions of people through her book, a book that shows her strong belief in faith and hope.

Following the 9-11 calamities, President George W. Bush in his State of the Union Address urged the American people to perform "acts of kindness." We can each play a role in uniting our community, nation, and world. We need to reintroduce kindness in order to help each other, especially during difficult times.

We can each play a role in uniting our community, nation, and world.

2004 was a difficult year with the presidential election, the unrest in the Middle East, and how that's impacting us here. While we may not be able to solve the world's problems, we can control ourselves. In order to have peace and kindness in the world, we must first be kind and peaceful ourselves. Just as we must heal ourselves before we can heal others. Author Wayne Dyer in *The Power of Intention* says, "You feel good not because the world is right, but your world is right because you feel good."

To paraphrase Wayne Dyer, we become what we think about. If we think about what's wrong with the world and how angry and fearful we are, then we'll act out on those unkind thoughts. In order to reach the power of intention we must not be offended by the atrocities of the world. Act to eradicate the world's problems but stay in peace. Remember at all times that, "what you think and do affects other people." Mahatma Gandhi once said, "We must be the change we wish to see in the world."

Mishaps are lessons our souls yet need to learn in order to heal. We all have areas in our souls that need healing. Someone else's healing need is different from yours and, therefore, we cannot judge the event taking place. We simply must consciously do what we feel is most "right" in our hearts. "The road to your soul is through your heart."

Mishaps are like knives that either serve us or cut us, as we grasp them by the blade or the handle.

—James Russell Lowell

Peace Pilgrim says, "It is an orderly universe, and the suffering that comes to us has a purpose in our lives—it is trying to teach us something. We should look for its lesson."

We can learn from our own mistakes, but we can also learn from the mistakes of others. We can live compassionately to create positive energy. Or, we can choose to act out in a cruel manner, in which negative energy is produced.

You can continue this energy by exploring possibilities of stepping out of your "comfort zone." When you do this, you are able to make incredible progress. You move vertically, improving and growing with each step rather than getting stuck in your habitual patterns on the horizontal path of mundane, routine living. It is up to you to create the life you want. Script it as in writing your own chosen eulogy. You have your choice of the life scenes you want, and you have the choice of how to write your next act.

> You have your choice of the life scenes you want, and you have the choice of how to write your next act.

Exploring possibilities and getting deep with yourself and others requires openness and honesty. When you allow yourself to do this, your life becomes enriched. Exploring and living from your true good will allow you to connect in the most positive ways with people and events that society puts before you.

Connecting with Others

To be fully human is to be fully connected with those around you and with society. "You receive from the world what you give to the world." If you intentionally show anger and hatred toward another, then that energy is reciprocated unto you. Remember, if you were to write your own eulogy, what would that be? How would you act toward others if you were living from your soul? Keep yourself in check and always act the way you would want to be treated. This is responsible living; it's a life that will make your spirit flow with incredible energy. Let down your guard and stop putting up barriers. When you feel fear, release it and replace it with positive thoughts and kind words.

To gain perspective, we need to understand love. Sometimes our life circumstances or our emotions prevent us from acting with love. When we can truly love ourselves, others, and the world, we affect the daily transactions of our lives in a healthy and positive way. When we are faced with a difficult situation in which it seems difficult to be kind to others, we need to think of love as power. Not a controlling power but a gentle flow of energy. Instead of choosing to hate, judge, or manipulate others, choose to love. If someone betrays you or acts unkindly, your choice to love will allow you to find a positive solution to the problem.

> I promise you will notice a difference in your life that's most buoyant, positive, and fulfilling.

No matter what our past life experiences are, it's never too late to learn how to give love, show love, and act in loving kindness. When you live this way, I promise you will notice a difference in your life that's most buoyant, positive, and fulfilling.

When I went to a car dealership to buy a slightly used car, I erased from my mind the image of the "typical" used car salesperson. I ended up having the best car-shopping experience of my life. I walked in with no barriers and connected immediately with my salesperson. We went outside on the hottest day of the year (97 degrees) and I felt completely at ease. At the first car he showed me, I immediately said, "Oh, it doesn't have a sunroof and that's what I'd like." I didn't allow my energy to get drained listening to a spiel on a car in which I knew I had no interest. At this point, I told him the max that I could spend on a car (I was on medical leave and was financially strapped). When you're upfront, true, and respectful to yourself, it's amazing the respect you get in return. I was extremely kind to him, knowing that he was doing his job, but I always made sure he knew honestly where I was coming from. I had the most enjoyable test drive in the car with no fear of "he's trying to sell me this car." I was sincere and genuine with my feelings and then reiterated again my financial dilemma. He and his manager crunched numbers to make this happen for me. I knew I had received an unbelievable deal because I'd already done my homework by checking the blue book for that car, same year and similar mileage.

The tone of voice and expressions I used made a big difference. When you don't bicker with someone, but honestly tell them what you're looking for and why, the end results are positive. When it seems that someone is being overbearing or perhaps attacking you, stop and take a look at your own behavior and actions. You could be instigating that negative energy. When you win over people with kindness, everybody wins in the end. I did not feel drained, as I have with past car shopping experiences, because I was only there a short time. I didn't allow myself to fall into spiel after spiel. In return, my salesperson had one of his quickest sales because he simply met my needs, instead of trying over and over to coerce a sale. We both experienced a sense of peace and harmony.

We experience peace and harmony when we live through love and wisdom versus doubt and fear. We are able to give love, forgive, and focus on the good in others and in ourselves. Too often, we wait to express our love. Show others and tell them how you feel from the bottom of your heart today rather than waiting for a tragedy. This is how we grow and so may our relationships with others. Love aligns us with our personal power. Love is wisdom not weakness. We can set boundaries and say "no" when we need to without feeling guilty. When we think in terms of good for ourselves and others and see everyone as living in the same world, then we have a healthy sense of our own individuality. Our sense of self is based on love and not defensiveness.

Love is powerful when you choose to love because you respect yourself and others. When you love in this manner, you will get what you want with more ease and satisfaction. When you love from a place of fear, thinking that you will avoid a consequence or

> Love is powerful when you choose to love because you respect yourself and others.

in order to get what you want, then you are not being truthful and are not following your core values.

Love allows us to appreciate and show our gratitude and generosity, which connects us with others most genuinely. Our experiences flourish, and we become one with our environment.

At the end of Chapter II are quotes from many world changing leaders. We can each be leaders by living from our inner goodness and showing our own natural talents. In April 2003, author of *Life as a Daymaker: How to Change the World by Simply Making Someone's Day*, David Wagner embarked on a tour from New York to Los Angeles in a salon-equipped RV, offering free makeovers to people who needed them. Wagner is a world-renowned hair stylist, artist, entrepreneur, educator, and the owner of Juut Salonspas, the original Aveda salons. His employees consider themselves personally responsible for making their clients' days. Wagner deeply believes that if we make other people's happiness part of what makes us happy, we can then consciously begin to change the world. This is the heart of the Daymaking concept, and Wagner's mission. He sees himself as part of a revolution of inspired people who see the opportunity to change the world simply by making another person's day. While some lament the state of the world and fear what the future may bring, Wagner sees a planet on the brink of transformation. I agree with Wagner when he says "the world has more good than bad and that each of us has the ability to make the good bigger, while shrinking the bad. Kindness can inspire others, diffuse anger, bring hope, heal pain, and change the world."

Wagner made numerous stops to offer free makeovers to people who really needed some loving care: parents of children with cancer at hospitals and Ronald McDonald House, folks from local homeless shelters, fireman and rescue workers and others. All efforts were coordinated through local salons in each city.

Another person making a great difference with his skills is the founder of Walls to Bridges, Duane Lilja. "Our mission is to educate with the purpose of creating harmonious relationships between individuals and groups by knocking down walls of ignorance and building bridges of understanding. We are dedicated to contributing to a civil society where justice and respect prevail. We believe understanding and personal responsibility must be the underlying foundation to achieve these goals." Lilja does this by conducting seminars at high schools, colleges, and universities. Lilja is bridging the gap, uniting people of all backgrounds to see that the beliefs that lie in all of us have at least one goal in common. Participants are motivated to build their own framework of understanding centering on how similar cultures look at their fundamental belief about how people should treat each other. This common goal pertains to any belief or faith. Participants consist of anyone concerned with improving human relationships in business, educational institutions, or their communities. For more information, visit *www.wallstobridges.com*.

There are many organizations striving to increase humanity, integrity, and peace among youth and adults in the world. Here are several I found helpful. For teenagers, visit *www.challenge day.org*. For adults providing services to their community based on their unique talents, visit *www.passioninaction.org*.

When we give and are gracious, our lives run smoothly and peacefully. Kind acts will happen with more ease and others will automatically absorb and learn from our generosity and have respect for us. Having complete respect for one another is living with reverence.

Living with Reverence

Living our chosen eulogy is living with deep respect and reverence. Zukav in *The Seat of the Soul* describes the soul's perception as reverent and that each day we make the choice to carry out that perception or not. When our personalities are aligned with our souls, we perceive complete reverence. We have authentic empowerment and see all of life through our souls.

89

Approaching life with reverence requires the courage to live by your values and to live as your "best" spiritual person. So, when your spirit is challenged by those who deceive you by lying and acting out in hatred, you must have the courage not to drop to the level of living inadequately. When you allow yourself to engage in acts of kindness, then you will not feed yourself poison. You will remain reverent. Your soul will not accept the cruelty, jealousy, or lies of another person. Choose to act responsibly. When you choose to live in reverence, then you are able to forgive negative behaviors.

I was challenged many times by a co-worker who continually acted maliciously toward me. I can now see that those acts of jealousy were a part of her soul's healing and mine. She turned out to be a gift in challenging me to be reverent even when I could not fathom her cruel acts. Forgiving someone and living reverently lifts an incredible weight from your shoulders. You are able to fully enjoy life. You are not exerting your energy or wasting your time on negative situations. Living reverently is the true energy of the soul.

She turned out to be a gift in challenging me to be reverent even when I could not fathom her cruel acts.

Living truthfully is speaking truthfully. When you admit what is true and are able to speak it without the intention of hurting others, you are able to live with wisdom. This wisdom will provide a sound resolution to what was a problematic situation. When you forgive others, live truthfully and with reverence, you can feel the power of love, which ultimately gives you freedom. When you feel this freedom, you are able to make a difference in your life, the lives of others, and the world.

I used to live mechanically, always feeling as though I had to be doing something. While I felt like I was accomplishing something by giving of myself, I felt drained and unhappy. Giving needs to be real, natural, and genuine. Authentic empowerment is the natural energy of your soul. It is the being of your soul rather than the doing of your mind that tells you, "it's the thing to do." To live reverently is to live from your heart. It is to be patient, to love, and to honor all life forms. The soul evolves when it chooses to live with reverence. Living in your most reverent acts of kindness nourishes your body, mind, and spirit.

Kindness Nourishes Our Body, Mind, and Spirit

We continue to evolve as we focus on our intentions and live accordingly. We now see how our intentions affect the end result. "We see, for example, that a stick is a tool, and we see the effects of how we choose to use it. The club that kills can drive a stake into the ground to hold a shelter. The spear that takes a life can be used as a lever to ease life's burdens. The knife that cuts flesh can be used to cut cloth. The hands that build bombs can be used to build schools. The minds that coordinate the activities of violence can coordinate the activities of cooperation." (*Seat of the Soul,* Gary Zukav)

Rage can kill, but love and kindness nurture our bodies, minds, and spirits. Love is even more powerful, as it is the divine force that connects all of us. When we consciously tap into our energy of love and emanate that to others, they feel it and are healed. In turn, so are we. When we act out in loving kindness, it's a release of energy that makes us feel good.

My friend Debbie had taken in a foreign exchange student, Franz, who was kicked out of one family and was about to be deported back to Germany. This young man felt "saved," as he put it, and gave my friend a big hug. However, that was an act so that she would keep him for the rest of the year.

Debbie, who has twelve-year-old and seventeen-year-old boys, treated Franz like her own. Franz gradually changed, showing disrespect beyond belief toward everyone in her family

91

and toward her friends. He downloaded so many things on their computer that it not only affected the speed but eventually broke down the computer. When Franz wasn't on the computer, he was lying on the sofa. He refused to eat the dinners Debbie made and instead filled up on junk food and treats from the freezer. He talked back and argued constantly, making it very difficult to have a simple conversation with him.

I had tried a few times to talk with him about having respect for adults, but my words just went in one ear and out the other. He often bellowed about how much he loved America because he could do whatever he wanted. One night, I told him that while there are many opportunities here, a person still needs to have respect for others. Otherwise, others will not respect you in return, and that could lead to a miserable life.

I told him about the book I was writing, about acts of kindness and living your chosen eulogy. Enraged, he said that I couldn't force kindness down people's throats. He was right. I was so exhausted that I had felt my time had been a waste. But it was not a complete waste. Franz was actually a gift. He made me think about the approach of my book and that had I not argued back and simply shown him love, I would not have felt so terrible. My own defensive behavior was not nourishing my soul; instead it made my body tense and my mind race. This was not healthy at all.

> Enraged, he said that I couldn't force kindness down people's throats.

From then on, I continued to be kind to Franz as I always had, but if he became disrespectful or tried to start an argument I simply kept the conversation short or changed the subject.

My friend was so stressed out by Franz' behavior that she was counting the days before he had to go back to Germany. I told her that stressing was a waste of energy and that she should focus the goodness of her heart on her two sons. Sure enough, Franz suddenly wanted to spend time with the boys and the rest of the family, when before he had refused to be involved in any family functions.

Franz ended up being a gift in more ways than one. Debbie's sons, Dylan and Taylor, who had already been kind, respectful boys, became even more compassionate, considerate, and thoughtful of others. It was a joy to see how they had evolved from this situation.

At the end of the school year, Franz' parents flew out to America to pick him up. We all were delighted by Franz' parents, as they were incredibly compassionate, giving, and a joy to be with. They were open and initiated the conversation allowing all of us to genuinely express our feelings. We shared stories at an American style barbeque, and they took us out to a fine-dining restaurant. The weekend was filled with an incredible experience that none of us will ever forget. We all got along, including Franz, and continue today to communicate via email. We would all like to visit them in Germany one day.

Love always wins. While we can certainly learn lessons from pleasant and terrible situations, it is the acts of kindness that nourish our bodies, minds, and spirits.

Belitz and Lundstrom write in their book *The Power of Flow*, "Nurture your emotions. Feel them when they come up. When you're in the moment, you can have pain or anger or love or peace in all their fullness—then release these emotions and move on to the next moment and its requirements. This doesn't necessarily mean acting on your emotions: when someone rudely cuts you off in traffic and your anger rises, mentally explore your emotional triggers rather than tailgating their car."

While we can certainly learn lessons from pleasant and terrible situations, it is the acts of kindness that nourish our bodies, minds, and spirits.

The Game of Life

I've attended several workshops which made me stretch, think outside of the box, and test every part of my personality.

A trial game I vividly remember asked that all participants pretend they were on a ship in a big ocean. About twenty of us were "aboard," when the ship wrecked with no lifeboat and two miles from shore. What would you do? I recall saying that I would be certain that everyone could float on a piece of debris and that having once been a competitive swimmer, I would swim to shore to get help. People were absolutely appalled by my response saying that I was "righteous" in thinking only about myself. I later discovered that most people only heard part of what I had said.

This was an interesting game which led to yet another game in which the same group of people selected only five people that would continue to live. I had the lowest number of votes. The way people had perceived me from the previous game had made them think that I was not worthy to live. Telling someone you can or can't live made everyone in the group burst into tears, except for me. This response was another reason why I had the lowest number of votes. People did not perceive me as a compassionate, loving person. That night I cried long and hard. Earlier I didn't because I tend to hide my emotions in front of others.

Think about the ship wreck game and how you would respond. Then think about your everyday life with family, friends, and co-workers. Would your actions change? The game made me do an awful lot of thinking and soul searching.

You know the behaviors and situations that need to be changed in your life. Now it is up to you to do something about it. In Chapter I, you looked at the areas that were and weren't working in your home, work, relationships, and financial life. Think about those questions again and ask yourself now how you want to play the real game of life.

Ask what you need to know or do to resolve certain unsolved issues in your current life so that you can evolve when you move to the next level. Living a life based on positive intentional behaviors will be effortless. You'll see problems merely as stepping stones to the learning process of your soul. The sooner you choose the vertical path, the sooner you'll live with purpose and meaning.

You discovered your purpose or values during the unfolding of your soul in the last two chapters. Now it's time to keep your word and do it. Keeping your word means being committed and true to yourself and the promises you make. This comes with having faith and trust about everything you've learned so far and moving forward with confidence. Make sure that your promises are achievable. Start out with a few goals and accomplish those before setting out new ones. Live in the present, and you will be much more productive. Cramming too much now or worrying and scheduling too far into the future will hinder your performance. If you focus on executing your small promises, you will be true to your word. Then you will most efficiently and respectfully make a difference.

> To "kill" them with kindness is to "execute" your morals, values, and beliefs in a nonjudgmental way unto others.

In the game of life, "adversity" is very real. Accepting this and increasing the intensity or level of your spiritual practice will allow you to kill others with your kindness. To "kill" them with kindness is to "execute" your morals, values, and beliefs in a nonjudgmental way unto others.

Sometimes we get so wrapped up in our busy lives that we easily slip into our old patterns of mechanical living. In the final chapter of this book, you'll learn how to put your chosen eulogy in writing. Then, from time to time, you can refresh your memory on who you truly are and what you really have to offer this world. In the next chapter, you'll go even deeper into yourself and find what it means to give from the heart.

Key Points

- Detach yourself and look at situations objectively by not taking bad situations personally.

- Act in kindness even when misfortunes strike. Control your thoughts and actions. When you're in a rut, only you can pull yourself out.

- Think of all situations as a learning experience to help in your growth and to create possibilities in bettering your life and world.

- Exploring possibilities requires openness and honesty.

- Keep yourself in check and always act the way you would want to be treated by others.

- You will experience peace and harmony when you give love, forgive, and focus on the good in others and yourself.

- Love is powerful when you choose to love because you respect yourself and others. Don't choose to love in order to avoid a consequence.

- Approaching life with reverence requires the courage to live by your values and to live as your best spiritual person.

- Your intentions affect the end result. When you emanate kindness, others continue the cycle of positive energy.

- Ask what you need to know or do to resolve (unsolved) issues in your current life so that you can evolve and live a purposeful and meaningful life.

- Keep your word and be true to yourself and others.

- Live in the present.

Gifts from the Heart

—Artwork by Artist Carol Dwyer Card

Your best potential and strongest power and inner wisdom comes not from your mind but from your heart. Your mind works as a tool to communicate that which is in your heart.

—Kian Dwyer

Chapter IV

Gifts from the Heart

*Anyone who proposes to do good must not expect
people to roll stones out of his way, but must accept
his lot calmly if they roll a few more upon it.*

—Albert Schweitzer

*You can always try to teach people to love you in
your style, but never expect anyone, no matter
how close, to read your mind and heart. Tell
them what you want. The investment you make
in surprise is often a hidden expectation that
brings disappointment. Better yet, buy yourself
your heart's desire. Don't turn special days into
tests of love. Take care of yourself in the style you
prefer—yours. Then, anything else you receive on
that day will seem like extra love that you can
enjoy without hurtful expectations.*

—Jennifer James

Do It Your Way, but Don't Expect Your Way

Throughout my life, I have had a compulsion to help, care
for, and give to others. And while most times it was genuine
and heartfelt, there were times when it wasn't. There were times
when I gave for a predetermined end result—I had a motive that
sometimes was conscious but other times subconscious.

Having been adopted from another country and living in
America where my unique ethnicity stood out, I tried to fit in. I
wanted everyone to like me and was constantly trying to prove
myself. I can remember soon after I was adopted, I would give
everyone in my family—especially my mother—back, neck, and

foot rubs. I was only seven years old, so I'm not sure how heart-felt that was. I know how grateful I was to be in a family that gave me so many new experiences such as new clothes, car and plane trips, and toys that weren't broken. I believe that it began from the heart, but when I saw how people seemed to "like" me, I continued to do it even at the expense of my own happiness. They would be amazed that my hands could massage for two hours straight, so I took pride in that and never wanted to show that I was tired. Over the years, I've grown out of that compulsion and now sincerely and genuinely give back rubs to make others feel good, which in turn makes my heart and soul feel nourished. I'm not doing in order to be "liked."

As I mentioned in the previous chapters, if you love yourself and care about yourself, then you are able to truly give of yourself to others. If you cannot do this, then you will not treat yourself kindly, and you'll resent seeing others being treated kindly. Some people have a fear of showing or giving love to others because they don't know how they would accept love in return, or they don't feel they deserve to be loved. It is important to be able to give love and to let it come in. If you give love as a martyr, then this is contaminated love that's not truly from the heart; it will come back to hurt you. When you connect with the energy of your soul, you will truly feel good giving to others. You will have devoted compassion where there's no feeling of guilt, remorse, anger, or sorrow.

> If you love yourself and care about yourself, then you are able to truly give of yourself to others.

Giving should come with no expectation of a return gift. A tremendous weight is lifted when you live more authentically and are free spirited. You may have heard that if you don't forgive someone, it's like carrying around a twenty pound sack of potatoes every day. Well, if you're always giving in hopes of getting something in return only to be disappointed over and over again, that weighs you down and saps your energy. Remember, living the "good" life comes from within your heart and soul. When you are good and true to others, so shall it be unto you.

It's important, too, that we do not become judgmental when we don't receive what we expect. It's human nature to have expectations, but we must live from the perspective that the soul does not judge others even in situations we cannot fathom. If we participate in judging and hating others, this creates negative energy and throws off our balance. In order to be healthy and balanced (as we discussed in Chapter I), we need to continually fuel ourselves with positive energy. Remember that you can avoid many mental and physical illnesses by being aware of what's fueling you.

In fourth grade, I used to spend my allowance money on tons of candy, giving it away to kids at school so that they would include me in their circle of friends. However, the constant teasing—calling me "carrot nose" and "blacky"— remained. I wanted so much to be liked by them, and yet I didn't like them myself. How could I if I didn't like myself first?

> I wanted so much to be liked by them, and yet I didn't like them myself. How could I if I didn't like myself first?

Throughout high school, I felt a calling to help those with special needs, i.e., slow learners, kids with ADHD and autism. That patience and deep care was a true gift within my soul. To help those less fortunate kids was a form of giving that was healthy.

College, however, was another story. I worked extra hours at a coffee shop to help my roommate have spending money for her spring break trip. The $400 loaned her was never paid back. Later, I discovered that not only did her parents pay for her trip, but they gave her $500 spending money.

Years later, I still hadn't learned my lesson. I was taken advantage of in job after job, giving up what I wanted in order to be loved by others. At one point, I endured a co-worker's malicious acts over a several-year period. I wanted her to accept and like me so much that I was always friendly toward her. The malicious acts continued. Just before I went on medical leave I was betrayed by another associate who stole several of my clients. Those two people created a huge loss for me financially, physically, and emotionally.

Today, my soul thinks differently. I see those two co-workers as enormous gifts. For one thing, no one can make me physically or emotionally ill. What others do unto me is my choice, and I suffer the consequences or reap the benefits. Had I been true to myself and lived from my heart and soul, then I would have felt positive energy in return. I allowed myself to continue to be around negative, hateful people who drained my energy. Of course, I felt the repercussions of that. My focus was on them and their revolting acts rather than what I could create by focusing on me. And yet, I preached to new sales people to have a positive focus and not hang around negative people because of their ability to drain and sap their creativity and energy.

I'm sure many of you have stories of times when you have done something special for someone and did not receive even a thank you in return. This is a test that your personality needs to learn in order to heal your soul. It is important that you are a kind person, and when someone else isn't, it is **his** or **her** issue. It is something that **his** or **her** personality needs to learn in this lifetime in order to heal a part of **his** or **her** soul. So, do not take things personally when someone does not acknowledge your good deeds. When you live this way, it's amazing how you are able to give more naturally and receive massive abundance. Your positive energy is a magnet to those with the same energy. Ultimately, you will be at peace with yourself.

In the book *Soul Stories,* Gary Zukav writes, "If you give only what is easy to give, you can't grow. Share things that are important to you. You have to care about people to do that. This is the kind of sharing your soul wants to do."

When we break away from our old experiences, we are able to join the greater whole. We follow our hearts; contributing to the whole becomes our purpose. When we come to know ourselves, we can trust ourselves, our higher power, and others. We find risks energizing and our focus clear. We see others and events surrounding us through new eyes.

Should you feel tension about someone, take a deep breath and let it go, remembering that love always wins. Being nice means a lasting finish. When you give from the heart, you cannot lose because there are lessons you learn; those who may not be receptive at the time also learn from it. They may or may not show what they've learned in this lifetime, but that is not your concern. You created positive energy which sends that through another person whether that person is good or bad. Don't let the bad ones weigh you down. In this way, you'll have the energy to touch thousands more people who can then carry that positive energy to thousands more. This is what I call the gift chain or contagious giving.

The Gift Chain

Each year, I participate in the Breast Cancer Race for the Cure. Remember my angelic friend Cindy, the breast cancer survivor I wrote about in Chapter II? Well, in the 2003 Race for the Cure, I could not participate due to the surgeries I had for my avascular necrosis. However, there was a gentleman, Mo, who returned from the race with gifts for me. One item was a pink bracelet with the pink ribbon charm symbol for breast cancer. He said he wanted me to have the pink bracelet. When I asked him if he was sure about that, he said, yes, because the guys teased him about wearing it. I, in turn, gave it to Cindy's eight-year-old son, who said, "I think my mom would appreciate it more." So he gave it to his mother, who said that she had a party she was going to in which she had gifts for everyone but one of her nieces; that bracelet would be the perfect gift for her. Her son Parker then replied, "This is getting to be routine." That routine or contagious giving brought about the name "the gift chain."

The gift chain concept is what I call "World Help." Peter is someone who has contributed in this way. He is promoting world peace and is a link to the world help chain. He began by giving a handmade doll to another person with the condition that it would be passed onto someone else as a gift and so on. Each person who receives it must commit to get it to the next destination and report back to the preceding participants on the progress. For many countries, the Internet makes communication and tracking effortless. The idea was to get connected with others from different countries, and have the peacemaking doll travel around the world. You can take it from state to state, then country to country. The more hands that touched the doll, the greater the energy flow. Imagine the feeling of the person who receives it after thousands of others have received it as a gift. Knowing the miles it has borne and the countries it has trekked makes this a very special doll. The doll may have been torn and mended along its journey, but its strong gentle spirit remains. With what kind of gift can you start a chain?

Another example comes from Dr. Kristen Brown, who has been in the Peace Corps and continues to provide aide to underdeveloped countries such as Jamaica, Africa, and India. These countries, too, have hand-crafted dolls, but they sell them so that their people can have food, shelter, medical facilities, and education. With the help of individuals from the Jamaican government, the United States, and Japan, a group of rural women in Jamaica now have the means to become self-sufficient. These women are single mothers who live in poverty but are trying to feed their children. The crafts they produce are made of one hundred percent Jamaican materials. The crafts have many themes, such as a series of cloth dolls supporting the theme of education in Jamaica. The group of crafts-women is supported by community leaders and government and international agencies such as the Embassy of Japan and Land O' Lakes. Dr. Brown and these agencies are striving to enhance the welfare of the members in a community that is not necessarily their own. In July, 2003, Land O' Lakes helped the Jamaican women set up a website for their crafts (www.highgatedollsandcraft.com) so that people worldwide can join in this worthy cause. Many have contributed to this chain, and I now pass it on so that the chain will continue. The dolls you purchase can start another chain.

The gift chain is easy to start and doesn't have to be expensive or, for that matter, a material item at all. The gift chain creates world value and makes the planet radiate (ooze) with positive peaceful energy. It's the same type of concept as Oprah's kindness chain.

Beyond Material

Joy has nothing to do with material things or with a man's outward circumstance...a man living in the lap of luxury can be wretched, and a man in the depths of poverty can overflow with joy.

—William Barclay

Being grateful for what we have is experiencing true joy. We are able to experience inner joy when we give freely to others. When we see all that the world has to offer and are thankful from the bottom of our hearts, then we are able to understand meaning and our purpose. Our minds are at ease; we share our emotions; our spirits soar.

After reading the previous three chapters, you should feel quite grateful for who you are. Now you'll want to share your gratitude. You may at times come across a situation that makes you feel ungrateful. Focus not on the situation but on yourself and how you were feeling, acting, and responding before the event took place. Were your body, mind, and soul properly fueled? Were you not appreciative or living in a full state of gratitude? We experience joy when we live the full power of gratefulness every day, as if it's a way of life.

In the great land of America, we can easily take things for granted. We have a vast array of toys, from high-speed computers to lavish cars to palatial homes. What happened to the spiritual things? My great aunt Orena complained about her aches and pains for years, but in her final six months of life in a nursing home she suddenly was drawn to nature, as if she were seeing it for the first time. There was a certain calm and peace about her as she looked out of the window every day. She took note of the changing trees and the strength of the wind. She especially enjoyed the sunsets, appreciating the fullness of it as if each were the last. We take our universe and our relationships for granted. We need to give our full attention to our relationships with family, friends, business partners, significant others, and random people and acquaintances. We need to go beyond materialism and to give spiritually.

> We need to go beyond materialism and to give spiritually.

It is not possible for your soul to completely emerge if you place significance on artificial needs. These kinds of needs—bigger and more expensive toys, cars, and houses—drain your energy and ability to create from your higher self. Love is the best and most crucial gift of all. Without love, our minds cannot create, our hearts ache, and our souls diminish. If we do not give love to others and to the universe, how can we be fulfilled and replenished?

Eventually, we all die. But why not experience joy and happiness while we're here? It seems that people don't see or appreciate the simple things in life until they are faced with death. Imagine how dynamic our lives would be if we became alert to the unfolding of the universe. There are people who are so hungry for love that they accept material things as a substitute. No matter how much money or how many things we have, we will never have the true feeling of love. With love comes tenderness, gentleness, and compassion. Compassionate giving illuminates love to others and the universe. Our bodies are here to experience love and to extend love. This journey is a realm of devotional awareness by which we examine the meaning behind our experiences and then gain the spiritual power to endure.

Generosity is sharing the essence of your inner core—the angel in you. Start the cycle of giving love to others, and you will feel and see a radiant world before you, one that will give you complete inner joy. When you give of yourself, you will experience and manifest joy. Living your chosen eulogy emanates out to everyone around you. They cannot help but take in the joy and compassion themselves, which enlightens them and gives them the capacity to carry it out to others.

There are many gifts of love you can create to initiate your chain of kindness. This can be a rich exchange of vital information. Even though I used to work in a straight commission sales environment, I always wanted other salespeople to flourish. If another salesperson needed help with product information, handling a customer complaint, or needed to increase his or her service scores, I would help him or her.

I loved it when people asked me questions because it kept my mind fresh so that I could be even more productive. I enjoyed helping other salespeople succeed because then they would be happy and it would make for a healthy work environment. Who wants to work around sour people? I looked at the picture of the whole company and knew I had invested stock in the company. If you help others succeed, in the end, you become more fruitful as well. Everybody wins.

If everyone operated this way, there wouldn't be wild rages of jealousy. "Cut-throat" and "ruthless" salespeople would not be words in our vocabulary. If people opened up their hearts and were more compassionate and giving toward their co-workers, bankruptcies could be prevented. Giving more of yourself creates colossal rewards in return.

A New Meaning to "Re-Gifting"

Some of you may have received a gift that didn't suit you, so you gave it to someone else. This is not a bad idea when it is done sincerely and from the heart. I have received gifts that I couldn't use at the time but I kept them because of the thought behind them. Later, I discovered how very much I did need that gift. A year or two down the road, you, too, may suddenly have a dire need for an unwanted gift. Or, you may come across a situation wherein someone else could benefit from the gift. You "re-gift" it to someone who has a real need for it. Peace Pilgrim says we should not get attached to material things. Once we don't find them useful we should give them away to benefit others. Then we would be free—we wouldn't burden ourselves with things we don't need.

Enjoy the Game, Give the Prize

Another example of "gifting" is giving away the prize. I used to do this every year at the State Fair. Enjoy the game, but give away the gift. There was a particular game I was really skilled at, and I would consistently win a mammoth stuffed animal. I enjoyed the challenge of the hand-eye coordination, along with the systematic approach of the game. I took in the pleasure of the game and gave away the gift to a child. I had no need for a gigantic elephant, gorilla, or polar bear, but I had the skill to attain one every time. Why not put a smile on a young child's face, especially one that doesn't own many toys. The gratitude will be yours as much as theirs.

From Age One to One Hundred

A mother's heart is the child's schoolroom.

—Henry Ward Beecher

Truthfulness is a cornerstone in character, and if it be not firmly laid in youth, there will ever after be a weak spot in the foundation.

—Jefferson Davis

You can instill thoughtfulness and giving early in a child's life whether you are a parent, teacher, mentor, sibling, or friend. The concept of sharing and taking turns is common and taught by many of us. What we don't do as often is teach the concept of giving through emotion, actions (behavior), and speech. Give a warm hug and say "I love you." Love and affection are wonderful gifts that we all need. We can be good role models as adults by introducing compassion and love as soon as we can to our young ones. In turn, they will make an enormous impact in our world when they become adults.

We, along with the universe, must evolve. We don't have to simply recite that crime rises each year and that it's more heinous and that these violent acts are starting at younger ages. Instead, we should notice all of the achievements being accomplished by the youth at younger ages than before. The number of people educated has also increased dramatically over the past century. Be aware and focus on the positive and that's what will continue.

When we choose to live consciously, with courage and compassion, we have the choice to turn things around. We are not bettering ourselves or the lives of others or the world if we just tune out. We need to embrace and be aware of what is unfolding before us, not dwelling on the things we cannot change. Rather, we should concentrate on those things that we can impact. We may not be able to solve the world's problems but we can control ourselves and our actions. By improving our thoughts and actions we influence the people around us. Then we can transform the world one step at a time.

You can make a difference simply by taking small steps in changing your way of thinking: replacing fear, negativity, and pessimism with love, compassion, and generosity. You can be magnanimous no matter what the contribution. Every piece of the puzzle is essential. You have something desirable and useful within you.

You can volunteer at homeless shelters, hospitals, nursing homes, or special needs organizations for kids or adults. As you share yourself with others who are in need, you will experience warmth in your heart and soul. You'll experience a powerful energy. As you help others, they, in turn, will be helping you to live from your deepest authentic self.

When we become responsible (authentic) and are honest with ourselves, then we are introducing more honesty into the collective consciousness of the world. We can build from this enlightened foundation. Honesty is a path that leads to happiness. Would you like living in a world where everyone is as honest as you? The dishonesty you encounter in the world is a reflection of your own pretense. We need to assume ownership for the world's dishonesty. We are all dishonest as long as we do not compassionately work to correct the dishonesty of the world.

Would you like living in a world where everyone is as honest as you?

As you get older, you need to make sure you continue your awareness and compassion. You cannot stagnate. You must continue the vertical path in order to feel joy and purpose in your life. Compassionate living is healthy living. There are many ways to increase your generosity whether you're a child, teenager, young adult, middle-aged, or a senior. Make a list of ten different things you can do to help others and then perform something from the list each week. Some examples may be babysitting, yard work, carpooling (you drive), or tutoring. Think about what you could use help with or would enjoy receiving. Give that to others. For example, if you enjoy massages and you know someone who has a stiff neck or sore back that could really benefit from it, then offer to give one.

> Make a list of ten different things you can do to help others and then perform something from the list each week.

According to an analysis by the University of Michigan (published in *Psychological Science,* 2003), older adults who give to others live longer than those who do not. The analysis goes on to say that "people who are generous in their help of others reduce their short-term risks of dying by sixty percent." The analysis was funded partially by the National Institutes of Health. Four hundred older couples participated in the University of Michigan's Changing Lives of Older Couples program. The couples were chosen randomly in 1987 and were tracked for the following five years, and again recent evaluations were completed.

> Older adults who give to others live longer than those who do not.

Living from the Heart

As he thinketh in his heart, so is he.

—The Bible, Proverbs 23:7 KJV

"The road to your soul is through your heart." In Chapter I, you did your soul discovery to learn what your personality (body) is on this earth to achieve. You dug deep into your daily thoughts to find what inspires you and what your true hidden talents were. Your thoughts and values are based on your choices. You cannot let others or your environment or society determine those for you.

Now, dig deeper and let what you've discovered emanate through your heart. In Mitch Albom's book *Tuesdays with Morrie,* Morrie—who's dying from Lou Gehrig's (ALS) disease—says, "What really gives you satisfaction is offering to others what you have to give." What he meant was giving of your time; for example, going to senior centers to share your stories with the elderly and to listen to their stories in return. Teach a particular skill, like computers, fitness, art, or music.

There are so many things you have to offer. Even small talents may have vast meaning for someone else. Some people just need your time, patience, and companionship. Go beyond the money or material objects. Morrie says about finding a meaningful life, "Devote yourself to loving others, devote yourself to your community around you, and devote yourself to creating something that gives you purpose and meaning." He goes on to say, "Do the kinds of things that come from the heart. When you do, you won't be dissatisfied, you won't be envious, you won't be longing for somebody else's things. On the contrary, you'll be overwhelmed with what comes back."

Focus on and create good intentions. If your gut says something doesn't feel right, then don't do it. Be in tune with your emotions. Without awareness of your emotions, you are not able to experience reverence. In *Seat of the Soul* Zukav writes, "Reverence is not emotion. It is a way of being, but the path to reverence is through your heart, and only an awareness of your feelings can open your heart."

To be reverent, we need to allow ourselves to open up to our family, friends, and the rest of the human population. Express your feelings with them and hear what they feel. When you have the courage to do this, your heart becomes more powerful and compassionate. You grow from the result of your interactions.

You become invigorated and your heart energized. When you distance yourself from your heart and treat others with distance or badly, then you suffer. We heal ourselves when we treat others with compassion.

Zukav writes, "Trust allows you to give. Giving is abundant. As you give so it shall be given to you. If you give with judgment, limitation and stinginess, that is what you will create in your life— judgment, limitation, and stinginess. What you say to others shall be done exactly unto you." If you radiate love and compassion, you will receive it. If you radiate fear and suspicion and a sense of wishing to keep people at arm's length, then negativity comes to you because that is what you are asking for.

Trust in your heart. When you have the courage to give from your heart, the results are astounding. The universe is always providing for the needs of your soul. Allow the guidance of your inner wisdom that teacher's voice to free you from your fear and enjoy your interactions with others. You will create harmony within yourself and around you. When you give out of kindness and the goodness of your heart, with no motive, you will feel no pain in your heart. You will move up the vertical path in abundance and joy.

Think of the concept of living your own chosen eulogy. You hope that people will show up for your funeral and will say kind words. Yet, you don't consciously think, talk, and act out in your most generous ways right now. You draw up your will to include all of the special things you want to give to your loved ones, yet it would be so much more meaningful to give it to them now. Doing kind acts throughout your life and giving from the heart is living your chosen eulogy.

> You draw up your will to include all of the special things you want to give to your loved ones, yet it would be so much more meaningful to give it to them now.

This does not mean that you have to worry about your future. Consider the consequences and be accountable for the choices you make each day. If you're living consciously and responsibly every day, you keep your energy powerful.

Do not worry about tomorrow, but live in the now. Eckhart Tolle in his book *The Power of Now* explains, "Full attention is full acceptance, is surrender. By giving full attention, you use the power of the Now, which is the power of your presence." Be in touch with each moment you are living and you will be living with authenticity and integrity.

Let your intuition guide you, and you will automatically operate from an empowered heart. Your intentions should be from your heart rather than your mind. Your truth is in your heart and your fear is in your mind. Divine intelligence is in the heart.

Living from your heart means living consciously and in complete awareness and trust. You may not have expected some of the outcomes of your experiences but know that it was appropriate and meant to be. Whatever happens was perfectly and precisely what was to be. If you realize this, you will naturally make the best choices in your life, which will contribute to the evolution of your soul. This is the conscious path to authentic empowerment. The path you walk is your choice. If you choose to learn through anger, then that is what you will feel and receive incessantly. If you choose love and live from your heart, then you will experience being loved by others.

Now how does your heart want to live? What do you want to contribute to the universe? As you dig deeper within your true self, does the verbiage of your chosen eulogy shift? Do you know what your heart desires? So often, people think that going with your heart rather than your mind is irresponsible behavior. Quite the contrary is true. Your best potential and strongest power and inner wisdom comes not from your mind but from your heart and soul. Your mind works as a tool to communicate that which is in your heart. Your mind can also act as a barrier in letting your true inner gift shine. What a waste and what a shame. It's up to you to choose the most positive behavior in any given moment. If you set your intentions according to your heart, you align your personality with your soul. Move up the vertical path to experience the light and you will feel empowered, secure, and fearless. You create the reality that you experience.

> You create the reality that you experience.

Giving Throughout the Year

If you live each day not knowing what tomorrow will bring, you are living your full potential and literally enjoying your life completely each day.

Part of living through your heart and staying connected to your soul is what and how you choose to give throughout your lifetime—throughout each year, month, week, or day.

"We make a living by what we get, but we make a life by what we give."

—Winston Churchill

Write It, Say It, and Show It

The key to creating a friendlier world is taking the time to make it a friendlier world. We can actively do this each day by saying it, writing it, and showing it. These habits will feel so incredible that you'll want to do them all year long.

"Today, I act from my heart. I take the extra seconds to be warm and gracious with those I meet."

—*Transitions*, Julia Cameron

Write It...

One of my favorite things to do is create a special album for a special friend, family member, or significant other. It can consist not only of photos but of poems that you've written yourself or ones that you have found meaningful written by others. Writing poems happens to be one of my delights, but you can always write a letter or just a few words. If you cannot think of the right words, look through a magazine and cut out words that pop out at you that fit with your relationship. An idea for a birthday gift is to write a list of adjectives showing the fine qualities of your loved one that equals the number of the person's age. So if your friend is turning forty, make a list of forty words that describe how you feel about the person.

Say It...

Words that come from the heart enter the heart.

—The Sages

You can also take what you've written and say it. In person. You can sing it if you'd like. Make spontaneous phone calls throughout the year and when you ask someone how they are doing, really mean it and listen! Compliment others, whether it's a stranger you pass or the waitress at a restaurant, or your doctor, teacher, salesperson, friend, family member, or co-worker.

> Make spontaneous phone calls throughout the year and when you ask someone how they are doing, really mean it and listen!

Show It...

You can plan a surprise event that can be a week long or a day. Oftentimes people do something extra special for the fortieth, fiftieth, and sixtieth birthdays and so on, but what about the years, months and days in between? If you know that the person you're gifting likes to travel, then plan a surprise trip. They may enjoy going for walks, so plan a special outing to walk beautiful trails, hike a mountain, or simply walk along the beach. Perhaps it's fine dining, music, a play, an art museum or an amusement park, or zoo that is his or her favorite. Experience these special events **with** your friend or family member.

Another idea I've practiced since I was seven years old is to make a certificate of a service I'd like to provide. For me, it was giving a coupon saying "one free back rub," "one free foot rub," etc. You could do one for a sister, brother, or friend that says, "A night of babysitting little Joey and Sally." Or how about coupons for cleaning a house; organizing an office, room, or entire home; doing laundry; pet sitting; or cooking? Think of what you're best at (most skilled in) or enjoy most—and give it. If these are services you'd rather pay to have someone else do, then give a certificate from those places.

There are unlimited ways to make a difference in people's lives. The best gift can be done with our time, energy, money, possessions, food, understanding, listening, advice, knowledge, and the list goes on and on. Become aware of the needs of other people. Read people's facial expressions, tone of voice, and body language. Being a good listener takes practice. As you master the art of listening, your own life becomes meaningful, significant, and enriched. Listening to someone is a great act of kindness. Remember a time someone was interested in listening to what you had to say. Remember how good it felt. Remember the specific details that indicated to you that you were being listened to. Think of three people who would especially appreciate your listening to them. Go out of your way to find opportunities to build up your listening skills as you build up your compassion. Sometimes simply listening can be the best gift of all.

The Best Gift

I believe the best gifts come from personally giving of ourselves. However, sometimes giving a unique gift, certificate, or a class toward fulfilling someone's passion or dream can be a wonderful idea.

Take the time to fit the gift to the person. Whether it's for a family member, friend, significant other, or business, personalizing the gift creates a moment that will long be remembered. It doesn't matter if it's for a specific holiday, wedding, birth, or graduation. Taking the time and effort shows your appreciation toward that certain person and reflects your thoughtfulness. An engraved gift is just one idea of many that will send a heartwarming message.

Here's a list from *Surprise Gifts (www.surprise.com)* which can help you find the best gift for the person for whom you're shopping. This is at least a good start, but you may have to dig deeper by asking yourself to describe the person you're gifting with one word. What would that word be? What are his or her hobbies? Does he or she have kids or pets? Does he or she like to travel, read, or take photographs? Is he or she into games, computers, or restaurants?

- **A Little Bit Country**
  Country western dance class
- **Always Cold**
  Portable heater
- **Appreciates Beautiful Things**
  Tropical flowers or plants

Gift list provided by Surprise Gifts—www.surprise.com

- **Avid Reader**
  First edition or rare book
- **Backpacker or Camper**
  Headlamp
- **Basketball Fan**
  Glow in the dark basketball
- **Bath Connoisseur**
  Spa gift baskets
- **Bicyclist**
  All-in-one bike tool
- **Birdwatcher**
  Night vision scope
- **Boater**
  Navigation products
- **Cabin Fever: For the Snowbound**
  Classic board game
- **Caffeine Fiend**
  Coffee art
- **Can't Come Home for the Holidays**
  Holiday video, miniature Christmas tree
- **Canoer, Kayaker**
  A paddling trip and lesson
- **Caregiver to a Loved One**
  Maid Service
- **Cat Owner**
  Feline birth stone jewelry
- **Celebrating Aging**
  A theater subscription
- **Cheese Connoisseur**
  Cheese-making kit

Gift list provided by Surprise Gifts—www.surprise.com

- **Chocoholic**
  Chocolate-of-the-month
- **Christian**
  Subscription to a Christian magazine
- **Christmas**
  Holiday concert tickets
- **Commuter**
  Emergency road kit
- **Cross Country Skier**
  Electric footwarmers
- **Crossword Puzzler**
  Crossword puzzle club
- **Dating Again**
  Car wash service
- **Divorcing**
  New address labels
- **Dog Owner**
  Puppy pager
- **Empty Nest**
  Dinner for two
- **Environmentally Responsible**
  Banana paper stationery
- **Fine Arts Lover**
  Original art
- **First Car**
  Car wash kit
- **First Computer**
  A computer class
- **Fishing**
  Portable chair

Gift list provided by Surprise Gifts—www.surprise.com

- **Football Fan**
  Customized jersey
- **Frequent Flyer for Business**
  Portable DVD player
- **Gardener**
  Flower bulbs
- **Genealogy**
  Membership in *Ancestry.com*
- **Getting Older**
  Handyman services
- **Golfer**
  Mouse driver
- **Hanukkah**
  Dreidel
- **Has a Bad Back**
  Support cushions, yoga class
- **Has the Blues**
  Comedy CD
- **Hates to Cook**
  Dinner delivery
- **Hiker**
  Portable survival kit
- **History Buff**
  Antique maps and prints
- **Hockey Fan or Player**
  NHL goaltender mask telephone
- **Horse Rider**
  Magazines about horses
- **In Graduate School**
  Book annotation kit

Gift list provided by Surprise Gifts—www.surprise.com

- **In the Military**
  Freeplay hand-powered radio
- **Jewish**
  Historic tree
- **Kwanzaa**
  Encyclopedia Africana
- **Likes Hand-made Things**
  Native American baskets
- **Likes Spicy Food**
  Sam McGee's hot sauces
- **Likes the Mountains**
  Walking stick or pole
- **Lives a Healthy Life**
  Body-fat scale
- **Lives in a Small Apartment**
  Hanging pot rack
- **Loves a Pet**
  Pet grooming services
- **Loves to Cook**
  Custom apron
- **Loves to Travel**
  Traveler's book light
- **Martial Arts–Karate**
  Comfortable lounge pants
- **Model Builder**
  Display case
- **Movie Buff**
  Movie script
- **Musician**
  Tickets to an orchestra

Gift list provided by Surprise Gifts—www.surprise.com

- **Muslim**
  Quran software
- **No Sense of Direction**
  Compass, maps
- **No Time to Spare**
  Dinner delivery
- **Off at College**
  Prepaid phone card
- **Oprah Fan**
  Subscription to *O* magazine
- **Organic Only**
  Body care products
- **Pet Bird Owner**
  Talking tutors
- **Pet Fish Owner**
  Tank-cleaning service
- **Photographer**
  Acid-free boxes
- **Quilter**
  Vintage fabrics
- **Recently Retired**
  A session with a personal trainer
- **Runner**
  Illuminated safety belt
- **Scrapbooker**
  Scrapbooking magazine subscription
- **Sews**
  Leather sewing bag
- **Spacenik**
  Space society membership

Gift list provided by Surprise Gifts—www.surprise.com

- **Spiritual but not Religious**
  Zen rock garden
- **Stamp Collector**
  Stamp album
- **Stocking Stuffers**
  Scratch-off lottery tickets
- **Stressed Out**
  A trip to a day spa
- **Walker**
  Pedometer
- **Works at Home**
  Phone headset

Gift list provided by Surprise Gifts—www.surprise.com

Go the Extra Thank You

God gave you a gift of 86,400 seconds today. Have you used one to say "thank you?"

—William A. Ward

We can be thankful to a friend for a few acres, or a little money; and yet for the freedom and command of the whole Earth, and for the great benefits of our being, our life, health, and reason, we look upon ourselves as under no obligation.

—Seneca

For as long as I can remember, I have said, written, and shown my gratitude to others. Perhaps this naturally came as I was so grateful to have been taken away from an unhealthy environment and adopted into a family where I had many opportunities. My mother said the reason why she and my father chose me was because I was always deep in thought, sitting on my haunches in the corner by myself, and observing those around me. They said I was quiet and reserved compared to the other wild, screaming children. My mom said the orphanage was not an environment that would contribute to the growth of my soul.

How grateful I am for all of the soul-searching and growth that's been afforded me here in America. This immense gratitude I expressed throughout my life by thanking my friends, family, teachers, co-workers, bosses, waiters, salespeople, clerks, orthopedic surgeons, and the list goes on and on. I've said it and I've written special thank you notes. Not only would I give to my co-workers and managers during the holidays but throughout the year, whether it was for a kind act received or simply for being there.

When I managed a carpet store, I felt tremendous joy working with a group of skilled men. I'd give them all matching ties, or surprise them with pizza or Asian food. I'd give them an extra long break or let them leave early, showing my thanks for a job well done. Of course, I earned their respect and received the highest productivity in the history of that sixty-year-old company. When you give to others and do your best, others want to give their best in return.

> When you give to others and do your best, others want to give their best in return.

Many people are grateful only when good things happen. When tragedy strikes, we need to look at what we have rather than what we don't have and express our gratefulness.

Give a thank you note to those who least expect it. Thank those special people who have made life easier and more enjoyable. Remember to give a thank you with no expectation of anything in return and you will be surprised by the astounding service you receive. When you go the extra thank you, others tend to go the extra mile for you.

Sometimes life gets so busy that we don't always thank peo-
ple for the things they do. So for every time it has gone
unspoken...this is just to let you know that what you do
never goes unnoticed, and it's really appreciated.

—Americangreetings.com, Inc.

A simple thank you goes a long way. In order to write an authentic "thank you," you first need to be truly grateful for what you have. Make a list of all the things, events, people, services, and places for which you are grateful. By realizing what you have, your gratefulness will bring you a joy that you will automatically want to pass on to others. Make Thanksgiving every day of the year, and practice gratitude through each word, thought, and action you display.

Many people and places would love to receive a thank you note or letter such as:

- people who perform favors for you, such as babysitting, giving you rides, delivering fresh produce;
- people who took the time to interview you for a job;
- people who "mentor" you by sharing their knowledge and ideas with you;
- your parents, friends, and significant others;
- your co-workers, management, and assistants;
- organizations such as hospitals, retail operations, and restaurants; and
- people who give you gifts.

"Gratitude is the appreciation for kindness. The more we
are thankful for, the more we will find to be thankful for."
—(Louise L. Hay's book *Gratitude, a Way of Life*.)

When you are truly grateful and thankful, you will feel joy in your heart. When you feel this joy, it makes it easy to write a thank you. A simple thank you does not mean a quickly written one with little thought or emotion; an authentic thank you is written from the heart.

Here are ways to help you write from the heart:

- Focus on who you're writing to and make it personal. Be specific and mention something that would only apply to the person. For example: the person's favorite hobby, food or pastime.

- Focus on the gift, event, or gesture by mentioning it. For example: "I can't wait to have my first dinner party so we can use the new china."

- Write from your heart; share how you feel about the gift or gesture, and talk about the appropriateness of it. For example: "Your babysitting for my kids has truly been a lifesaver during these difficult times."

Writing a thank you connects you to others. You share your humanity, and it feeds your soul. The best time to write a thank you is when the gift or event is fresh in your mind; you are closest to your emotions, your responses are sincere, and they have a personal touch. The rule of etiquette is to mail out thank you notes within two weeks of the event, gift, or favor. However, the sooner the better as most people appreciate your immediacy. For example, a consumer may come back to make another purchase with you after receiving your thank you rather than going to a competitor. In many cases, mailing your thank you within 24–48 hours is good practice (for example, following a job interview).

We can set a good example for our youth by teaching our kids how to write thank you notes early in their life. They will learn to appreciate the kindness of gift giving and giving from the heart. Take the kids along when you're shopping for thank you cards and have them help you pick them out. Have the kids make and write thank you cards with you. Toddlers can draw a picture and as they get older they can go from a sentence to two sentences and so on.

Here are some guidelines to make it more enjoyable:

- Have on hand colorful paper, markers, pens, stickers, rubber stamps, and paint.

- Turn on the music or TV (on low volume) and don't make it seem like homework.

- If there are many notes to write, spread them out over a week, so that resentment doesn't arise.

- Take an active interest. If they get stuck, help them compose the note or create the drawing.

"Time is made up of captured moments. The things we share and the moments we spend together will become gifts that my heart won't ever forget."

—Flavia

Key Points

- Giving comes with no expectation of something in return.

- When you give from the heart, you cannot lose because there are lessons you learn. Those who may not be receptive at the time learn from it too.

- Start a gift chain.

- You experience joy when you live the full power of gratefulness every day as if it's a way of life.

- Go beyond materialism. It is not possible for your soul to completely emerge if you place significance on artificial needs.

- "Re-gift" to someone who really has a need for something you've received.

- You can instill thoughtfulness and giving early in a child's life whether you are a parent, teacher, mentor, sibling, or friend.

- You have the choice to turn things around when you choose to live consciously and with courage and compassion.

- As you get older, you need to continue your awareness and compassion, which creates a longer life.

- Coming from within is based on your values and not what others determine for you.

- Focus and create good intentions. If your gut says something doesn't feel right, then don't do it.

- Doing kind acts throughout your life and giving from the heart is living your chosen eulogy.

- Let your intuition guide you, and you will automatically operate from an empowered heart.

- Part of living through your heart and staying connected to your soul is what and how you choose to give throughout your lifetime.

- Take time to fit the gift to the person by personalizing it and finding out what's meaningful to the person you're gifting.
- Look at what you have rather than what you don't have. Express your gratefulness.
- Write a thank you from the bottom of your heart.

Living Your Chosen Eulogy

—Artwork by MaryAnn Millay

Living your chosen eulogy...choosing to live your most honorable self by following your heart's desire to live life with purpose and meaning based on your values.

—Kian Dwyer

Chapter V

Living Your Chosen Eulogy

*Only those are fit to live who do not fear to die;
and none is fit to die who has shrunk from the joy
of life and the duty of life. Both life and death are
parts of the same Great Adventure.*

—Theodore Roosevelt

*Someone should tell us right at the start that we
are dying. Then we would be more inclined to live
life to the limit every minute of every day.*

—Michael Landon

Now that we've come to understand who we are and the difference we want to make in this world based on our core values and beliefs, I present to you my final chapter...Living Your Chosen Eulogy.

Accept Death

Before we can live our chosen eulogy, we need to accept death. In *Tuesdays with Morrie*, Mitch Albom writes about his former professor's final months of life and quotes him as saying, "Accept what you are able to do and what you are not able to do"; "Accept the past as past, without denying it or discarding it"; "Learn to forgive yourself and to forgive others"; "Don't assume that it's too late to get involved."

Morrie died from Lou Gehrig's disease. In an interview with Ted Koppel before Morrie's death he said, "When all this started, I asked myself, 'Am I going to withdraw from the world, like most people do, or am I going to live?' I decided I'm going to live—or at least try to live—the way I want, with dignity, with courage, with humor, with composure." No matter how much Morrie suffered every day he would get up and say, "I want to live."

Morrie had what he called a "living funeral" where he invited friends and family to his home. Each of them paid tribute to Morrie and filled the day with thoughtful, kind words. Living your chosen eulogy is a similar concept. Why wait until a funeral to express such love? We can show our love with acts of kindness and warmth in how we speak and interact with each other today and every day. Living our chosen eulogy is living with compassion for ourselves and others.

Don't wait until it's too late. An accident could take our life at age ninety, thirty-five or fifteen. Brian Moore of Ohio was just seventeen years old when his car went off the road and struck a utility pole. He emerged from the wreck unharmed but then stepped on a downed power line and was electrocuted. His parents found an essay that Brian had read days before his tragic death in 1997. He had shared the touching story titled *The Room*, by Joshua Harris, in front of his friends in his school's Fellowship of Christian Students. After his death, friends and family shared it with others, mistakenly calling it Brian's work.

The Room was originally published in the spring 1995 *New Attitude* magazine, two years prior to Brian's death. Since Brian's death, Harris says the article has made it onto the Internet reaching many people who would not have read *New Attitude*. Through his website, *newattitude@sitgracenub.org* Harris says, "One of the most gratifying experiences for me has been to hear of the article being spread with the byline 'Author Unknown.' My name was lost as it was passed along. This is the way our humble service for God should always be—we decrease so that He can increase. The original article is here online. I invite you to use it and distribute in any way you feel led to. It belongs to God." Here's Harris' vision on what Heaven is like described in his essay:

The Room

In that place between wakefulness and dreams, I found myself in the room. There were no distinguishing features except for the one wall covered with small index card files. They were like the ones in libraries that list titles by author or subject in alphabetical order. But these files, which stretched from floor to ceiling and seemingly endless in either direction, had very different headings.

As I drew near the wall of files, the first to catch my attention was one that read "Girls I have liked."

As I drew near the wall of files, the first to catch my attention was one that read "Girls I have liked." I opened it and began flipping through the cards. I quickly shut it, shocked to realize that I recognized the names written on each one. And then without being told, I knew exactly where I was.

This lifeless room with its small files was a crude catalog system for my life. Here were written the actions of my every moment, big and small, in a detail my memory couldn't match. A sense of wonder and curiosity, coupled with horror, stirred within me as I began randomly opening files and exploring their content. Some brought joy and sweet memories; others a sense of shame and regret so intense that I would look over my shoulder to see if anyone was watching.

A file named "Friends" was next to one marked "Friends I have betrayed." The titles ranged from the mundane to the outright weird. "Books I Have Read," "Lies I Have Told," "Comfort I Have Given," "Jokes I Have Laughed At." Some were almost hilarious in their exactness. "Things I've Yelled at My Brother." Others I couldn't laugh at: "Things

135

I Have Done in My Anger," "Things I Have Muttered Under My Breath at My Parents." I never ceased to be surprised by the contents.

Often there were many more cards than I expected. Sometimes fewer than I hoped. I was overwhelmed by the sheer volume of the life I had lived. Could it be possible that I had the time in my years to enact each of these thousands or even millions of cards? But each card confirmed this truth. Each was written in my own handwriting. Each signed with my signature.

When I pulled out the file marked "TV Shows I Have Watched," I realized the files grew to contain their contents. The cards were packed tightly and yet after two or three yards, I hadn't found the end of the file. I shut it, shamed, not so much by the quality of shows but more by the vast time I knew that file represented.

When I came to a file marked "Lustful Thoughts," I felt a chill run through my body. I pulled the file out only an inch, not willing to test its size, and drew out a card. I shuddered at its detailed content. I felt sick to think that such a moment had been recorded. An almost animal rage broke on me.

One thought dominated my mind: "No one must ever see these cards! No one must ever see this room! I have to destroy them!" In insane frenzy I yanked the file out. Its size didn't matter now. I had to empty it and burn the cards. But as I took it at one end and began pounding the floor, I could not dislodge a single card. I became desperate and pulled out a card, only to find it as strong as steel when I tried to tear it. Defeated and utterly helpless, I returned the file to its slot.

Leaning my forehead against the wall, I let out a long, self-pitying sigh. And then I saw it. The title bore "People I Have Shared the Gospel With."

The handle was brighter than those around it, newer, almost unused. I pulled on its handle and a small box not more than three inches long fell into my hands. I could count the cards it contained on one hand.

And then the tears came. I began to weep. Sobs so deep that they hurt. They started in my stomach and shook through me. I fell on my knees and cried. I cried out of shame, from the overwhelming shame of it all. The rows of file shelves swirled in my tear-filled eyes. No one must ever, ever know of this room. I must lock it up and hide the key. But then as I pushed away the tears, I saw Him. No, please not Him. Not here. Oh, anyone but Jesus. I watched helplessly as He began to open the files and read the cards.

I couldn't bear to watch His response. And in the moments I couldn't bring myself to look at His face, I saw a sorrow deeper than my own. He seemed to intuitively go to the worst boxes. Why did He have to read every one? Finally, He turned and looked at me from across the room. He looked at me with pity in His eyes. But this was a pity that didn't anger me. I dropped my head, covered my face with my hands and began to cry again. He walked over and put His arm around me. He could have said so many things. But He didn't say a word. He just cried with me.

Then He got up and walked back to the wall of files. Starting at one end of the room, He took out a file and, one by one, began to sign His name over mine on each card. "No!" I shouted, rushing to Him. All I could find to say was "No, no," as I pulled the card from Him.

His name shouldn't be on these cards. But there it was, written in red so rich, so dark, so alive. The name of Jesus covered mine. It was written with His blood. He gently took the card back. He smiled a sad smile and began to sign the cards. I don't think I'll ever understand how He did it so quickly, but the next instant it seemed I heard Him close the last file and walk back to my side. He placed His hand on my shoulder and said, "It is finished."

I stood up, and He led me out of the room. There was no lock on its door. There were still cards to be written.

This essay was written from Harris' religious context and vision of Heaven.

Through Harris' essay, many have been able to accept death. Accepting death means living spiritually. Living spiritually means seeing the importance of all aspects of life. Realize that every one of us and everything that occurs in our world is significant. We must choose to open our eyes and face the truth about ourselves and within our world. We must engage in our surroundings and play our part in making the world a better place for all to live. We all know that we will die someday but many of us live in so much fear that we don't want to believe it. Part of being able to live life fully is accepting death. When we know we are going to die and are prepared for it, we can be more involved by living each day to its fullest. As Morrie said, "Once you learn how to die, you learn how to live."

It seems that many of us do not experience the world fully until we are faced with death. I'm an example. I was constantly on the go, thinking that by keeping busy I was accomplishing something. I was not fully aware of my surroundings and the beauty of the world. I did not fully connect with people or appreciate their role on this planet. I was faced with a near-death situation in 1994 when an abusive ex-boyfriend pushed me into a bee hive. I'm allergic to bee

> It seems that many of us do not experience the world fully until we are faced with death.

stings. Had a friend not driven me to the hospital when he did, I would have died. The doctors said I was ten minutes from death. After this experience, I left for four days on a retreat by myself to the North Shore of Lake Superior. There I purged. I became one with the waves and the sea gulls. I was swept away by the gentle breeze as words blew into me. I wrote, and wrote, and wrote until I couldn't write anymore. After all of this cleansing, I was ready to get out of the abusive relationship and start living. We are human, though, and make mistakes. Soon, I chose to go back to what was familiar. I still had lessons to learn and years of healing. After six years, I finally left him for good.

In January, 2003, I was diagnosed with idiopathic avascular necrosis. This is an incurable bone disease wherein the blood does not flow through the bones, so the bones disintegrate. All those years that I kept going unaware of what was happening to my body, I was really avoiding taking good care of myself. This lack of consciousness made the disease worse. I was not in tune with my own body. The pain progressed each year until this disease got to a stage four. So far I've had surgery on both feet and both knees. The disease can spontaneously affect other bones. I cannot sit, stand, or walk very long. Every morning when I wake up, I'm stiff from the osteoarthritis that has set in, along with osteopenia in my hips, arms, and back.

I have chosen to accept what I can and can't do. I've embraced this change and life. Now, instead of listing all the things I can't do, I recite, "Look at what I can do today." I am thirty-eight years old and do not want to wait until I'm the "big forty" to say I better think about experiencing life. It's never too late to get involved and to make a difference. It's never too late to give to the world and show your innermost values and talent. When you accept that you could die anytime, then you may see that "living the good life" means living from your authentic self...the energy of your soul. This

> Instead of listing all the things I can't do, I recite, "Look at what I can do today."

139

energy is so powerful that I feel as though I can move mountains and fly with the birds. In reality what I—and you—have to offer is even greater than that.

As long as we can love one another and live from the goodness of our hearts every day, then there is no reason to fear death. When we give love, we feel love in return and we can die without feeling unfulfilled. When our bodies die, our souls live on. Our spirits and love remain in the hearts of everyone we touched. Imagine the choice you have in creating all that love.

Once we come to the realization that death is peaceful, we can start living with peace of mind. So, as September 11th hero, Todd Beamer, said, "Let's roll!"

In the previous chapters, we've discovered who we truly are on the inside and how to let the best part of us come out naturally. We learned about our values and the difference we can make in this world by living from our authentic selves. Now, each day, we need to keep asking ourselves: Am I living the way I want to? Am I being the person I want to be? Am I doing everything I need to do to nourish my mind, body, and soul? Am I living from my heart? Am I accepting death and living each day at my highest level of wisdom and consciousness without worrying about how the future unfolds? One way to be true to your commitment is to put it in writing.

> Am I living the way I want to? Am I being the person I want to be?

Write Your Own Chosen Eulogy

Throughout this book you've been connecting with your deepest inner self, and now you're ready to let your true self grow in your everyday life. Writing your own eulogy plays an important role in fulfilling your dreams of being the best you can be. The process of writing brings to the surface who you really are and what you value. By putting your thoughts on paper and sharing them, your eulogy becomes a gift to others and yourself. Writing your chosen eulogy is a positive experience which will allow you to accomplish what you really want.

Former president Ronald Reagan in his first year of presidency (1981) was thinking about how he would want to be remembered and had written letters showing how he wanted to better the world. He also had lists of prominent people who he thought were good people and would want to make a positive difference in this world. Reagan was a consummate story teller. We all have stories to tell. This book shows how to tap into our heart, to create passion, and to make our journey most meaningful today. The tools are here to preserve your own unique story.

Write down your feelings, experiences, passions, humor, and lessons learned throughout your life. Make this habit meaningful by writing from your heart. If you're having trouble starting to write, ask friends and relatives for their recollections and stories of what touched them the most about you and your character traits. What lies in their memories and what they cherish describes the goodness they see in you—the authentic you. Who have you been to people? For what do people tend to come to you? What role do you play...a nurturer, leader, mentor, motivator, mediator, or individualist?

Write about the things that truly make you happy. What inspires you? What do you want others to remember most about you? What are your finest qualities? Be honest and compassionate and write as many positive phrases as you can. You can begin your eulogy with a favorite quote, anecdote, philosophical inspiration, or statistic. Write your eulogy from the vantage point of the life you want to have lived and continue living today. Each morning, look at what you've written and

> Every night before you go to sleep, read your eulogy—the statement of who you truly are—and ask: Am I living what I believe?

ask: How can I live my life today in order to become this person? Every night before you go to sleep, read your eulogy—the statement of who you truly are—and ask: Am I living what I believe?

Writing in general, whether it is a eulogy, a letter, poem, or a journal entry is therapeutic. It can help bring out the truth and your innermost desires. Writing brings up memories, rekindles certain feelings, and helps you put your values into perspective. You may want to simply think about the idea of your eulogy and go to bed with a notebook beside you. You may write at night or when you wake up in the morning. Some people are more creative and inspired at night whereas others are "morning people." Each night or morning, write down your thoughts and feelings. You can cover anything from complaints, dreams, frustrations, ambitions, fears, etc.

This is merely a rough draft; it's good to release your negative feelings so that you leave room in your heart and soul for more positive energy. Write about your life's dreams or regrets. What would you do differently? Brainstorm your goals and create a type of grocery list. Think about your immediate wants and needs and how to create a better life for yourself and others. What contributions would you want to make? There are no rules on how your eulogy should be written since it's your chosen eulogy. Let whatever is on your mind flow onto the paper.

The power of writing is undeniable and there is no better time than now to take advantage of it. This eulogy does not have to be perfect since you may make changes throughout your life as you grow and your aspirations change. The important thing is to have something down in writing to show your commitment to making a difference in this world. Start today. Embrace the day. Give of yourself in order to bring light into our world.

Here's a condensed version of my chosen eulogy...

Kian's an avid reader and a collector of quotes. A few of her favorites are: Albert Einstein's "I think and think for months and years. Ninety-nine times the conclusion is false. The hundredth time I am right." Vince Lombardi's "The harder you work, the harder it is to surrender." And Henry Ford's "Failure is only the opportunity to begin again more intelligently." She acknowledges that after twenty-nine years of failures, at the age of fifty-one, Abraham Lincoln was elected President of the United States. Carrying these quotes and thoughts with her for years illustrates convincingly her life story. Persistence and perseverance describe this courageous lady, Kian Dwyer.

There has always been great mystery in Kian. Even as a little girl, she locked away deep-rooted thoughts. Her profound thoughts were bottomless as she sat silently in awe of the resonance that penetrated her soul. She was a "people watcher" and multifaceted as she gripped new lessons. As an observer, she intensely captured and absorbed all she could. She exercised her mind and sensed a pressing need to unlock her heart and soul. Her exterior showed skills of order, detail, and proficiency. Looking beyond her efficient and organized character, her warm side showed her as a natural mentor and caretaker. She had love for all, yet kept others at arm's length.

She worked arduously for years while unconscious of her worth and inner truth. Others were inspired by her texture, yet found it difficult to get close to her multilayered being. She was on the go, with no time for family or friends. Her goal was to become financially stable so that she could follow her dream of helping those less fortunate. She occupied every minute of the day, leaving no time for engaging in the world...until one day when she was struck with an incurable bone disease. Needing several surgeries forced her to stop running and immerse into her spirit. She was once again that angelic little girl with so much inside her heart and soul.

As an adult, she was able to unlock her inner wisdom and showed her greatest potential. May it radiate into the universe and be captured by others to make this world a better place for all. This led her to write the book *Living Your Chosen Eulogy*. Through her writing talent, she wished to captivate as many people as she could so that they would unlock the goodness within and live from their hearts. She now lives the good life as she is conscious of her soul's needs. Her pressing values, untold for so many years, are now released as she chooses each day to be the best she can be to herself, others, and the universe. She is living her chosen eulogy.

Her pressing values, untold for so many years, are now released as she chooses each day to be the best she can be to herself, others, and the universe. She is living her chosen eulogy.

Start Living Your Chosen Eulogy

According to Lisa Beamer in her book *Let's Roll*, her husband and hero Todd Beamer (who was aboard United Flight 93 on 9-11-2001) was driven to succeed. Lisa notes in her book that at one point during Todd's life, he said, "This is real life right now. I'm not going to start living it after I accomplish a few more goals or get a few more dollars in the bank. I'm living today. My wife and kids are here right now, so I don't want to say, 'I'll just keep up this schedule until something cataclysmic happens, and then I'll be the person I want to be.' This is the only shot I have, so I better find out what's most important and then do it."

Those who live passionately teach us how to love. Those who love passionately teach us how to live."

—**Sarah Ban Breathnach**

Know in your heart that the vertical path is the most rewarding. Starting today with every meaningful and loving thing we do. Believe in the power of (your) spirit, and it will help you through times of fear, loss, and uncertainty.

—**Nick Bunick in** *Transitions of the Soul*

Sit quietly in a chair and close your eyes. Picture your funeral (the celebration of your body passing and your soul moving on) and focus on who's there and who's not. Now think about who would give your eulogy. Think in detail about what this person would say.

Are you doing what you will look back on with pride? Are you in a career you love? Are you contributing to society? Are you living up to your youthful expectations? If you died today, what regrets would you have?

If you died today, what regrets would you have?

It's easy for us to get so wrapped up in our busy lives that we don't see what's really important. We might look back at all we've accomplished…getting an education and going from menial jobs to a real career. Yet we are unhappy because we were chasing the wrong things. As Morrie said, "The way you get meaning into your life is to devote yourself to loving others, devote yourself to your community around you, and devote yourself to creating something that gives you purpose and meaning."

Look back at your life. If you were told that you had one month to live, would you have done things differently? What would you have done? How can you engage in the world with your hidden values? You've thought about it throughout this book, and you've written it down. Now it's time to unlock those deep-seated values. Living your chosen eulogy is living with purpose and having a meaningful life that will give you joy and inner peace. Living your eulogy is about improving your life.

Improve Your Life

Give us clear vision that we may know where to stand and what to stand for—because unless we stand for something, we shall fall for anything.

—Megiddo Message

I worry that our lives are like soap operas. We can go for months and not tune in to them, then six months later, we look in and the same stuff is still going on.

—Jane Wagner

Improve your life and you will improve the lives of others, be a part of the evolutionary process of the world. Living consciously in complete awareness of the teachers around you will teach you much needed lessons to improve your life. Be careful to not just be a "people watcher" as I was. Take what you see and hear and run it through your system of values. Then let your inner wisdom shine. Don't fear your intuitions. Live intentionally from your heart. Look at your full potential. Stretch yourself to be all that you can be. Believe in yourself and your values...they are from your soul, and they are your true calling.

In the previous chapters, you've explored the possibilities of you. Now, you can make the choice to accelerate that by exploring further your ideal-life scenario and what you really want. When you do this, you will naturally attract or become a magnet for what's best for you. Your life will start improving. "What's meant to be is up to me." What's meant to be will come with ease when you know who you are, what you want, and how to live each day intentionally. As you grow, your values and what's right for you may change. That's part of your evolutionary process.

Every day, ask yourself what's most important? Ask yourself what you would do if today were your last day? Live with love, responsibility, spirituality, and awareness as if it's your final day to make a difference. Thinking and feeling this way will allow you to continue to improve your life.

Your dreams and desires will come to fruition more quickly as a result of your new awareness. You will be able to manage your life with a lot less effort, and you will naturally get rid of old patterns and behaviors that caused you pain before. "Living the good life" means that you are able to listen to your inner wisdom and avoid making the same mistakes as in the past. You will learn lessons more quickly. You will intuitively be aware of the consequences of certain behaviors or actions and will stop yourself from re-creating the same mistakes.

> Live with love, responsibility, spirituality, and awareness as if it's your final day to make a difference.

Remember the exercises you learned in Chapter I with breathing and visualization? Then, in Chapter II, you got in touch with your physical, emotional, mental, and spiritual intuitions. In Chapter III, you explored possibilities and intentions. Chapter IV took that a step further by creating intentions from your heart which feel good in your gut. Now, it's time to master everything you've discovered by focusing on it every day. Make it your daily intentional plan.

I do my best thinking early in the morning and before I fall asleep. You may find quiet time in the middle of the day, while taking a walk or simply being out in nature by a creek, a field, garden, beach, or woods. Pick a time when you're in complete silence so that you can focus on your breathing. Visualize who you are, what you want, and what you want to be. This will motivate you to help create your intentions. Increase the time allotted for this each day. You will find that this solitude, this space to yourself, is a positive and healthy means of living your best life. Soon, you will look forward to and enjoy this retreat of deep relaxation. You'll soon find a personal sanctuary within your own home simply by going deep in thought.

I learned deep breathing and visualization when I was just fifteen years old in a workshop about the unlimited power of your mind. The above relaxation exercise, a form of meditation, combines your right and left brain. The energy of both hemi-spheres process and create your values and priorities. You have more clarity when your right and left brain work together at the same time. You will have more strength in your decisions. Your thinking is lucid, and there's order and purpose in your life.

I've learned over the years to get in touch with my intuitions, to be spontaneous and creatively organized. Don't fall into the trap of running a harried, frenzied, and frazzled life by trying to keep up with an unrealistic list of goals. When you think from a relaxed state of mind, you are able to get your priorities straight and live for the moment, your present life. Do not waste your energy worrying constantly about what tomorrow may or should bring. Live for today, and you will find more meaning as your life unfolds.

Remember your grocery list of values or actions for your written eulogy? Now look at that list and think about what you could accomplish if you made just one positive change a month. Start now. Make a difference each day and month by living your principles.

Your New Life

I resolve to live with all my might while I do live. I resolve never to lose one moment of time and to improve my use of time in the most profitable way I possibly can. I resolve never to do anything I wouldn't do if it were the last hour of my life.

—Jonathan Edwards

Yesterday is but a dream, tomorrow is only a vision. But today, well lived, makes every yesterday a dream of happiness, and every tomorrow a vision of hope. Look well, there-fore, to this day, for it is life, the very life of life.

—Sanskrit Proverb

In your new life, remember to ask if you are living compassionately and responsibly with yourself and others. You cannot undo what you've done in the past, but it's not too late to change. It doesn't matter how old you are. Every day is significant, and every day is an opportunity to better yourself and contribute to the world. Don't dwell on past mistakes; rather, learn from them and let them guide you toward making the right choices today. Don't wait to forgive yourself or others. Lifting that weight will allow you to be open, aware, and free. Really listen, see, touch, smell, and taste; but go beyond those five senses to your intuition and your higher self.

Approach life with reverence; think and act as a spiritual person. From this day forward, reexamine the way you treat each being, animal, and life event. Be kind to all life forms and respect the earth. Living beyond your five senses evolves your personality and your compassion. Acts of kindness will flourish. In your new life of authentic living, remember that your soul is patient and nonjudgmental. Be sure to create that through your personality.

You've learned how to improve your life by learning how to use the two hemispheres of your brain. That relaxed state allows your full potential and wisdom to emerge. You will naturally be more effective, efficient, and productive every day. You will live from truth and reality versus dishonesty and illusion. You will best express yourself by hearing and feeling your intuition and wisdom.

How will you express your purpose in both your job and your personal life? How will you change your behavior with respect to your interaction with others? What must change today for you to live your chosen eulogy? Before you act or speak, ask yourself if it will benefit you and everyone around you.

> How will you express your purpose in both your job and your personal life?

In *A Revolution in Kindness,* editor Anita Roddick provides excerpts about putting meaning behind a word we've used lightly...*kindness.* We need to go beyond the common meaning. It took the tragedy of 9-11 for our country to see not only the importance of the heroes we lost but to become heroes or "kind" people ourselves. We can all contribute to making this country and our world a better place in revolutionizing kindness. Let's not wait for another jolt of terror for us to become what we're meant to be. We can start a *lasting* chain reaction today that will carry out for generations to come.

In critiquing the book *A Revolution in Kindness,* Danny Schecter with *Mediachannel.org* writes, "This profoundly simple word 'kindness,' is a word we like to scoff at in our everyday, hard-hitting lives but fail to really take a moment to grasp its dimensions."

Let's redefine and reintroduce kindness in our lives. Random acts of kindness influence young people. If you are not a parent, then think of yourself as a mentor. It is critical that our youth are given the most positive energy and knowledge that come from our "best" selves, our positive beliefs, values, and morals. Imagine what difference you can make in a child's life, which, in turn, impacts our world.

Are you truly obtaining the outcome you desire between now and death? This is living your dash.

Are You Living Your Dash?

Linda Ellis of Marietta, Georgia is the author of "The Dash," a poem which has been heavily circulated throughout workplaces and the Internet. She wrote the poem after discovering a woman in her workplace was dying of cancer. The woman regretted how she had spent her life making a living instead of making a life.

We never know what we may be handed at any given time or day. In Linda Ellis' poem, the dash is that fragment of a line between the years of someone's birth and death. It's an accumulation of all of the person's accomplishments and fears. It's the bridge between birth and death.

The Dash
©1996 by Linda Ellis

I read of a reverend
who stood to speak at the funeral of a friend.
He referred to the dates on her tombstone
from the beginning...to the end.

He noted that first came the date of her birth
and spoke the following date with tears.
But he said what mattered most of all
was the dash between those years.

For that dash represents all the time
that she spent alive on earth.
And now only those who loved her
know what that little line is worth.

For it matters not how much we own;
The cars...the house...the cash.
What matters is how we live and love
and how we spend our dash.

So think about this long and hard.
Are there things you'd like to change?
For you never know how much time is left.
You could be at dash mid-range.

If we could just slow down enough
to consider what's true and real,
and always try to understand
the way other people feel.

And be less quick to anger
and show appreciation more
and love the people in our lives
like we've never loved before.

If we treat each other with respect
and more often wear a smile...
remembering that this special dash
might only last a little while.

So, when your eulogy is being read
with your life's actions to rehash,
would you be proud of the things they say
about how you spent your dash?

www.lindaslyrics.com

Over the years that I visited my grandpa in the nursing home, I never heard from him or anybody else residing there that they wished they would have worked more. I was always so proud of my strong work ethics and would boast to my grandpa that I got it from him. At ninety-two years of age, he had a despondent look on his face as he said that he wished he wouldn't have worked so much and would have spent more time with his family; he would have enjoyed life more. The look in his eyes had quite an impact on me. I immediately changed my work schedule to a 24-hour a week job-share position. I also tried to balance my life by being a teacher's aide at a preschool two days a week, and I continued to visit my grandpa once a week. I was also mentoring a seven-year-old with autism. And when I could, I was a volunteer to help those with fetal alcohol syndrome. I figured I had covered ages three to ninety-plus making a difference in many ways. Since my grandpa

Some of us may be able to change and start living our true values overnight, but most of us need to take steps daily and monthly to consciously live from our true good.

passed away, I've been spending more time sharing with family and friends.

Some of us may be able to change and start living our true values overnight, but most of us need to take steps daily and monthly to consciously live from our true good. We all are quite capable of making one change a month. Going for a hundred changes overnight would be unrealistic; we would be setting ourselves up for failure.

Keep in mind who you are and who you want to be from this day forward. You have already done a lot of the work; now it's time to contribute. When you become who you really are and feel it with your heart and soul, then your energy becomes a magnet. You attract the people and work which align with your values, leading you to your best life. This, of course, is your "chosen" life—the life you've always wanted but may not have figured out until now.

The website *PartnersinKindness.com* encourages people around the world to perform daily acts of kindness. "The reality is that everyone can learn how to increase his or her kindness skills." The website has many goals, including designing programs for schools, employers, and government agencies for the purpose of teaching kindness. Find out how you can partner by linking your purpose with others. Whether you're helping starving homeless people, teaching kids to read, or visiting the elderly at a nursing home, you are showing and giving "love."

In creating your new magnetic "successful life," let's look at the dictionary definition of "successful." It is defined as, "having obtained something desired or intended." Life is defined as, "the interval of time between birth and death." You've already discovered who you are; now you're ready to obtain your desired outcome for the period between your birth and your death— your dash.

Is Your Dash the Way You Want It to Be?

No matter what your religious beliefs, the question, "Did you live your life?" can be quite intimidating. It implies you have a particular life that you are supposed to be living and that any other life is false or not authentic. We do not want to be like many who wander through life plagued by the nagging suspicion that they are making up their lives as they go along. People who live in fear confine themselves. They seem unsure of who they really are and define themselves by the knowledge they have acquired or the achievements they have racked up along the way. By defining themselves in this way, they may become reluctant to change careers or learn new ways of doing things because then, in the new career, they would be forced to throw away their achievements. This could mean getting rid of their identities. But this identity is based on a false sense of values. It is based on habits. We are habitual creatures (beings) and habits are not easy to change. However, the exercises in the preceding chapters provide tools for changing our belief system. Changing jobs was not an issue for me as I did it quite often. I changed my career a few times and jumped from job to job in search of happiness and my true worth, only to end up unfulfilled every time.

Throughout the chapters, you've been able to discover who you are, your identity, and **your** inner values. Furthermore, you've learned not to be reluctant to investigate who others are. In learning about reverence, we do not generalize or define others by superficial markers such as their education, sex, or race. Our actions and ideas are not used as weapons, but rather tools for growth. We are not selfish. Our actions are based on inner wisdom instead of doubt or fear. We live by our standards and not according to what others expect of us. Living your dash means having no uncertainty, living your intentions, and not making up your life as you go along. Your successes and achievements are not accidental. That's the power of intention. Your wishes will miraculously happen. You influence every choice you make. Be careful not to fall back to your old roles. Challenge yourself to be present in spirit, not just in body.

Be conscious of your energy. Everything you do either gives you energy or saps it. Continue to be that magnet of positive energy. This way, you will continue to attract and be engaged in positive relationships and events. With practice, your new awareness will become a natural way of life. You will be able to discern whether a situation or a person is draining your energy or not. If you feel exhausted after being with someone or participating in a particular activity, then this impedes the dash you want to live.

> Everything you do either gives you energy or saps it. Continue to be that magnet of positive energy.

Are you living your life? That's your dash. Take a look at your professional and family life and ask if you're doing what your heart desires. Can you honestly say that you are "living" your dash? Are you attracting great opportunities? When you have positive energy, your life runs smoothly and is productive. When it's not, you'll know to take a look at what you're doing and change it. It doesn't help to panic or complain about it. Be true to yourself and you will recognize what needs to be done to pull yourself out of a rut. Breathe, relax, visualize who you are, your angelic mission, and become who you want to be.

You may know family members, co-workers, friends, or acquaintances who've been in the same job for years and complain repeatedly about how much they dislike their job. Not only do they thrive on bringing others down with them, they cannot possibly be living their dash the way they truly want to be. They choose to be stuck in their negative ways and not move up the vertical path of a meaningful and purposeful life. They may be falsely secure with what's familiar and afraid to step out of their hard, cold shell and into the warm, enlightening experience and euphoria of love.

Living from your soul is to be alive, breathing the good life. Living in pessimism and negativity is destructive. It's not living fully. Each day of nonconstructive behavior kills the positive energy with which you were born. Remember, there's an angel in you. When you choose to live your dash from your "angelic" viewpoint, there is nothing to fear between life and death.

The point of the poem is that your dash is what represents your life span. Your dash is now. You are living your dash. Live the dreams you had when you were young. Be alive in your heart. Your life will be guided by your own self-created, divine life purpose. You'll be on fire with passion and positive expectation when you awaken each day. Your heart will be filled with joy.

> You'll be on fire with passion and positive expectation when you awaken each day.

That dash is who you have been in your life. That dash is small, and it's now. It's not tomorrow, not when you have that other job, not when you get enough money, not when the kids are grown, and not when your best friend is reading your eulogy. You've been given today; there are no guarantees on tomorrow.

Your Dash Is Now

Eckhart Tolle in *The Power of Now* suggests, "When you surrender to what **is** and so become fully present, the past ceases to have any power. You do not need it anymore. Presence is the key. The Now is the key."

Here are some questions to help you determine what matters in your personal and professional lives and to recap your values from chapter one.

- If you were diagnosed with a terminal illness and you wanted to tell your children, or the young people to whom you are close, the three most important things that you've learned in your life, what would they be?

- What gives you the greatest joy, satisfaction, and renewal in your life, and how could you do more of it?
- Who are you without your job, your money? Describe in detail.
- What activities could you add to your life that would be sources of richness and joy?
- Think of someone you admire deeply and explain why.
- What do you need to start doing? What do you need to stop doing?
- How will you use your time and energy?
- If you could give the people of the world a gift, what would it be? What do you want for others?

It's time to take your discovery one step further and start expressing and living your purpose. It's time to convey your greatness. Start by making a firm commitment that you'll no longer settle just for what life offers you. You make the choice, and no one else can do that for you. You must take full responsibility for an amazing gift that was bestowed upon you at birth—the power to create your life as a work of art. You are the artist, and you are responsible for the colors (your actions) that you put on your canvas of life.

Living your purpose does not mean sitting back and letting the universe do it for you. "Rather, it's a partnership. Your part is to be open to whatever presents itself, to listen to your inner voice and respond to it, to put yourself out there, to do all you know to do, to contribute your part to the greater whole." (*The Power of Flow* by Charlene Belitz and Meg Lundstrom.)

> Living your purpose does not mean sitting back and letting the universe do it for you.

You have the realization of what's possible. Now use your wisdom to carry it out. You've always had the knowledge within you. With your new wisdom, you can tap into it with ease and let your intuition guide you. Act on your intuition, and follow your wisdom. Live consciously, and be aware of the needs of your soul. Don't ignore your chosen eulogy. Believe and trust your thoughts and feelings, and be committed to setting them forth. When you live consciously, you will not have false expectations. You have the control to make healthy choices to create what you want. If you start to question yourself, then ask your Higher Power, angel, God, Buddha, or whatever your affiliation may be. Then trust in the intuitive response you feel and go for it...take that leap of faith.

Make your spiritual development a top priority, and you will understand and fulfill your unique purpose on this earth. You will be a positive model for both the youth and other adults.

You will live life every day with meaning behind every action and word. You will be completely aware and notice every thought; you'll know and trust which ones to follow through with. You'll become aware of the meaning behind your daytime and nighttime dreams. You will be able to recognize and interpret life events with confidence, following your gut. You'll know to be patient with what you've learned, to not force results and to let the answers flow naturally in order to create the best outcome.

You'll also know that you don't need to know *everything!* Part of the joy in life is to experience and learn throughout your journey. When you trust yourself, you don't fear the unknown because your wisdom will propel you to make the right choices. When you feel like you're pushing, forcing, or second-guessing an outcome, then the timing may be off. When it's right, it won't feel hard to accomplish. You can be patient without procrastinating. From here on, you'll learn how to enhance your life, not complicate it. In the following list, look at your journey as something rewarding. This gives you ultimate freedom and a true feeling of being alive.

> You'll also know that you don't need to know *everything!*

- Live up to your standards.
- Carry out your promises.
- Make integrity your top priority.
- Look at what you have, not what you don't have.
- Ask for what you need.
- Be patient.
- Don't overreact to problems.
- Show your gratefulness.
- Create solutions by not pushing for results.
- Don't make excuses.
- Learn from your mistakes.
- Create strong relationships.
- Go beyond the material and nourish the internal you.
- Make conscious, responsible choices in everything you say and do.
- Show your love and care for people...be compassionate.
- Live with reverence (respect).
- Listen and be attentive to others and your surroundings.
- Keep your ego in check.
- Monitor your energy.
- Don't be judgmental.
- Explore your dreams and what you really want.
- Be aware of who you are being, not what you are doing.
- Listen to your inner wisdom, and follow your intuition.
- Live spiritually.
- Live in the present.
- Take time for yourself.
- Trust yourself.

- Live with intention.

- Live with purpose and meaning.

- Live your best life—your chosen eulogy.

Mihaly Csikszentmihalyi, author of *Flow, the Psychology of Optimal Experience,* writes: "The answer to the old riddle 'What is the meaning of life?' turns out to be astonishingly simple. The meaning of life is meaning; whatever it is, wherever it comes from, a unified purpose is what gives meaning to life."

If the camera were rolling, how would you be perceived? Be mindful of what you project. Everything occurs as a result of your intention whether you are with your family or friends, at the workplace or driving in rush hour traffic. Commit to making your life be exactly what you want it to be. When you do that, everything else will magically work out for you. When you orient your life around your values, the right doors will open for you.

You never know how long your "dash" is. Even if you're diagnosed with a terminal illness of two years, one year, six months, two months, you want to make the best of your time here.

We can step off the well-worn path into the lifestream of all possibility. Begin living the gift that is uniquely yours. Are you stuck in your old patterns? Do the beliefs in your mind match the values in your heart and soul? Are you aligning your personality with your soul? Are you living with intention in every action, thought, and feeling? Every cause has an effect. In living your dash the way you want, you are making the choice to participate in the cause. This cause is your calling and will automatically have an effect, an impact on you and your surroundings. You are responsible for everything you say, do, and feel.

> Do the beliefs in your mind match the values in your heart and soul?

Hopefully, this book has already made an impression and has initiated an influx of positive energy. Empower yourself to create harmony and love. Celebrate the courage you've shown in embracing the mystery of you, that true goodness within. Release **your** buoyant life values. How you live your dash from here on is in the intentions of your desires and your chosen eulogy. It's a continual process of change for the better. It's your life! It's now or never.

Key Points

- When we accept death, we can live spiritually and fulfill our unique purpose on Earth.

- As long as we can love one another and live from the goodness of our heart every day, then there is no reason to fear death.

- Ask yourself each day: Am I living the way I want to live?

- Be true to your commitment by writing your chosen eulogy and making those words a reality.

- Keep your wants and needs in check. Create a better life for yourself and others.

- Living your chosen eulogy is living with purpose and having a meaningful life that will give you joy and inner peace.

- Believe and trust in yourself and your values—they are from your soul, and they are your true calling.

- From this day forward, reexamine the way you treat each being, animal, and life event. Be kind to all life forms, and respect the earth.

- Are you living your dash? Are you truly obtaining the outcome you desire between now and death?

- Living your dash means having no uncertainty, living your intentions, and not making up your life as you go along.

- Your dash is now...you've been given today. There are no guarantees on tomorrow.

- Everything occurs as a result of your intention, wherever you are and whomever you're with.

- You are responsible for who you are and everything you say, do, and feel.

- Living your best life is *Living Your Chosen Eulogy*.

Poems

Release

I release my grip on the past
  Open my heart and soul
Accept the seeds the future casts
  May bring with it a toll
I release the past and bless it
  Turn with resolution
To the future let upon it
  See the consolation
Our Earthly personality
  Just artificial aspects of the soul
Serve their functions in our bodies
  To which it creates a new lifetime flow
Filled with experiences we choose to react
  Will create good or bad energy
However we must learn from it and stay intact
  For it to create more energy
We may consciously choose to release
  The quite painful pattern
It may reappear again to tease
  So turn on the lantern

Shed light on what you've learned
    That in order to release we must accept
Changes occur...we get burned
    Don't resist, rather credit your attempt
For recognizing our loss of power
    Gives us more clarity and control
For unpredictable tests of the hour
    External events we don't patrol
It's all part of your soul's healing
    This journey is required to be done
Only then will you be releasing
    Complete and whole to the heavenly one

—Kian Dwyer
June, 2003

Do It Now, Don't Let It Lie

In pursuit of living consciously
Partake in a living eulogy

What's my purpose in the world now?
Follow your heart and take a vow

To bear gifts of kindness throughout the year
Of loving acts to those far and near

Accepting death allows you to love
No fear of what's handed above

With each day let your true self shine
Continue to grow the gift vine

Gifts from the heart may be written
Of my dear one I am smitten

From the heart may be spoken or shown
Giving to others not just your own

Imagine the beauty of the universe
If all followed the above verse

We never know when we may die
So do it now don't let it lie

—**Kian Dwyer**
September, 2003

Reader Comments

*Some of the following names have been changed
to preserve confidentiality*

Jan: Kian, how fabulous that you dedicated this time of recovery "Tikkun Olam," that is Hebrew for "repairing the world." Regardless of the tradition from which one comes, the end is typically the same: how can we create a world that is better than the one into which we were born? I commend you for not only trying to do that with your own choices, but by hopefully persuading others to do the same.

Gary: It is wondrous how we don't realize how important all our actions are and how they reverberate through the universe. I really respect and appreciate the value of every small action and am thankful that I can be honest enough and kind hearted enough to spread goodness and success through the world.

Jay: It's just amazing how adversity can inspire. Certainly, in your case, this is true. As you've shown in your book, you're able to share the empowerment and wisdom you've gained from your challenges.

Sarah and Doug: Wow, Kian, sounds like you have made excellent use of your time. Congratulations on doing your part to make the world a better place...your beautiful smile and sweet disposition already helped do that!

Annette: Dear Kian, you have a gift, a drive and a talent for making what you do of extraordinary scope, quality, and significance.

A Conversation
with Kian Dwyer

*Some of the following names have been changed
to preserve confidentiality*

Sharon: I have actually done some written exercises on writing my own eulogy. I found that it was a bit of a depressing eye opener especially as I get older and still find myself reverting to old bad patterns.

Kian: Thank you for sharing your writing experience. I've gone through many emotions myself. I found that I couldn't even begin to write my book until I had purged by writing many poems first. The release worked though and I was able to write the book rather quickly. It is definitely an "eye opening" experience as you say. I have found the end results to be quite uplifting. As you mention, we may fall back into old patterns, since we are human. The positive approach occurs when we are able to live consciously, recognizing this and emanating the good within us regularly.

Amy: What is the definition of Eulogy?

Kian: Eulogy is a tribute (high praise) showing respect, gratitude, or affection. It's something that shows the worth, virtue, or effectiveness of the person. Conventionally speaking, a eulogy is a written expression in praise of another person, presented at a funeral or memorial service. Alternatively, I look at it as a celebration of one's life. Or, as described in my

169

book, it can be something you've chosen or written as a commitment: to carry out your true values which come from your heart and soul. *Living Your Chosen Eulogy* is choosing to live your most honorable self every day starting now.

Cammie: I find the concept of "world-help" in *Living Your Chosen Eulogy* very interesting. I am constantly trying to figure out my purpose and how I can make a difference in this world. I've gone through so many problems in my life, but with the help of this unique book, I am finally living and making a difference each day based on my values. It works! Thank you.

Kian: In Marlo Morgan's book *Mutant Message Down Under* she quotes an Aboriginal saying, "I knew they believed that Divine Oneness planned no suffering to any living creature, except what the creature accepts for itself."

Julie: I've always been pretty fortunate in my life, growing up in a financially secure family. However, I felt like I was wasting my life. I lived in a beautiful home, and the first car I owned was brand new. I had so much, yet I felt there was no meaning in my life. I realized that the people I admired most were the ones making contributions toward the welfare of others. I finally decided that I wanted to make a difference in people's lives and the world. I have been living by my word and commitment, and my life has made a complete turn around for the better.

Kian: What's my purpose? How can I make a difference? These are two of the most common questions I hear. There are unlimited ways to make a difference. The important thing is to tap into your inner core values and discover what your talents are. There are questions and exercises throughout my book, *Living Your Chosen Eulogy*, which facilitate the process of going from discovering yourself and your unique gifts to taking action and creating possibilities in the world.

It looks as though you have found and are presenting your true self values and are making a difference. We tend not to see the obvious. The answers are simple and lie within us. It is human nature to analyze and complicate things. We know all along what's right and wrong and what we're truly good at, but our fear or false sense of security holds us back. When we become aware of our behaviors and actions and live from our heart and soul, we then live out of love rather than fear. Fear is something that can creep back into our lives, but we can learn to manage that fear and move on.

Rick: I am reading your great work and am enjoying it a lot. Your words are so nicely selected that they roll along like a song.

Kian: Thank you, Rick! It means so much that you're enjoying it. I'm glad it flows like a song—I do like to sing. We're all capable of releasing our fears and letting our hearts sing. I am enjoying life and the "tune" or path I've chosen.

Bibliography
and Suggested Readings

Albom, Mitch. *Tuesdays with Morrie*. New York: Bantam Doubleday Dell Publishing Group, Inc., 1997

Andreas, Brian. *Story People*. Berkeley, CA: West Coast Print Center, 1997

Bach, Richard. *Illusions*. U.S. Dell Publishing, 1994

Ban Breathnach, Sarah. *Something More: Excavating Your Authentic Self*. New York: Warner Books Inc., 1998

Bean, John M. *PhB—The Professional Human Being: Profiting from Purpose*. Edina, MN: Beaver's Pond Press, 2004

Beamer, Lisa (Wife of 9-11 hero Todd Beamer). *Let's Roll!* Wheaton, IL: Tyndale House Publishers, Inc., 2002

Beck, Martha. *Finding Your Own North Star*. New York: Crown Publishers, 2001

Belitz, Charlene and Lundstrom, Meg. *The Power of Flow*. New York: Harmony Books, a division of Crown Publishers, Inc., 1997

Bender, Sue. *Everyday Sacred*. New York: HarperCollins Publishers, 1996

Blackburn, Simon. *Being Good*. New York: Oxford University Press Inc., 2001

Bronson, Po. *What Should I Do With My Life?* New York: Random House, 2002

Bunick, Nick. *Transitions of the Soul: True Stories from Ordinary People.* Charlottesville, VA: Hampton Roads Publishing Company, Inc., 2001

Cameron, Julia. *Transitions.* New York: Penguin Putnam, Inc., 1999

Chandler, Paul-Gordon. *God's Global Mosaic: What We Can Learn from Christians Around the World.* Downers Grove, IL: InterVarsity Press, 1997, 2000

Csikszentmihalyi, Mihaly. *Flow: The Psychology of Optimal Experience.* New York: Harper Perennial, A Division of HarperCollins Publishers, 1990

Cutler, Howard C.M.D. *The Art of Happiness: His Holiness the Dalai Lama.* New York: Penguin Putnam, Inc., 1998

Dalai Lama. *Kindness, Clarity, and Insight.* Ithaca, NY: Snow Lion, 1984

Dyer, Dr. Wayne W. *The Power of Intention.* Carlsbad, CA: Hay House Inc., 2004

Dyer, Wayne W. *Wisdom of the Ages.* New York: HarperCollins Publishers Inc., 1998

Dyer, Dr. Wayne W. *Your Erroneous Zones.* New York: First Avon Printing, 1977

Eadie, Betty J. *Embraced by the Light.* Placerville, CA: Gold Leaf Press, 1992

Grabhorn, Lynn. *Excuse Me, Your Life Is Waiting.* New York: Hampton Roads Publishing Co., Inc., 2000

Grant, Verlene. *Beyond Racism: A Deeper Understanding of Cultural Diversity.* Minneapolis, MN: Kirk House Publishers, 2004

Halberstam, Yitta and Leventhal, Judith. *Small Miracles.* Holbrook, MA: Adams Media Corporation, 1997

Hall, Doris & Ken. *Go Out and Live.* Edina, MN: Beaver's Pond Press, 2003

Hannah, Kristin. *Angel Falls.* New York: Crown Publishers, 2000

Havener, Cliff. *Meaning: The Secret of Being Alive.* Edina, MN: Beaver's Pond Press, Inc., 1999

Hay, Louise L. edited by Jill Kramer and designed by Jenny Richards. *Gratitude: A Way of Life.* Carlsbad, CA: Hay House, Inc. 1996

Heilbrun, Carolyn G. *The Last Gift of Time: Life Beyond Sixty.* New York: The Dial Press, 1997

Henricks, Gay. *Conscious Living: Finding Joy in the Real World.* New York: HarperCollins Publishers, Inc., 2000

Isaacs, Florence. *Just a Note to Say.* New York: Clarkson Potter, 1995

Jones, Shirley Ann. *Simply Living: The Spirit of the Indigenous People.* Novato, CA: New World Library, 1999

Kielburger, Craig & Marc. *Take Action! A Guide to Active Citizenship.* Hoboken, NJ: Wiley, John & Sons, Inc., 2002

Lamb, Sandra E. *Personal Notes: How to Write from the Heart for Any Occasion.* New York: St. Martin's Press, 2003

Lamb, Sandra E. *How To Write It: A Complete Guide to Everything You'll Ever Write.* New York: St. Martin's Press, 1999

Lewis, Barbara A. *Being Your Best: Character Building for Kids.* Minneapolis, MN: Free Spirit Publishing, Inc., 1997

Luhrs, Janet. *The Simple Living Guide.* New York: Broadway Books, 1997

McFarlane, Evelyn & Saywell, James. *If: Questions for the Soul.* New York: Random House, 1998

McGraw, Phillip, Ph.D. *Life Strategies.* New York: Hyperion Press, 1999

McGraw, Phillip, Ph.D. *Self Matters.* New York: Simon & Schuster Source, 2001

Miller-Russo, Linda & Peter. *Angelic Enlightenment.* St. Paul, MN: Llewellyn Publications, 1999

Mills, Roy. *The Soul's Remembrance.* Everett, WA: Onjinjinkta Publishing, 1999

Mills, William-Stewart. *Breakthrough: The Power of Conscious Conversation.* Edina, MN: Beaver's Pond Press, 2003

Morgan, Marlo. *Mutant Message Down Under.* New York: HarperCollins Publishers, 1991, 1994

Moore, Thomas. *Care of the Soul.* New York: HarperCollins Publishers, 1992

Obershaw, Richard J., MSW, LICSW. *Cry Until You Laugh.* Edina, MN: Beaver's Pond Press, 2004

Patton, Sue. *The Courage to Be Yourself.* Berkeley, CA: Conari Press, 1991

Phillips, Bob. *Phillip's Awesome Collection of Quips & Quotes.* Eugene: Harvest House Publishers, 2001

Pilgrim, Friends of Peace. *Peace Pilgrim: Her Life and Work in Her Own Words.* Sante Fe, NM: Ocean Tree Books, 1991

Regis, Jacqueline. *The Journey of the Good Samaritan.* Edina, MN: Beaver's Pond Press, 2004

Resnick, Stella. *The Pleasure Zone.* Berkeley, CA: ConariPress, 1998

Richards, M.C. *Centering in Pottery, Poetry, and the Person.* Hanover, NH: Press of New England, 1989

Richardson, Cheryl. *Stand Up for Your Life.* New York: The Free Press, 2002

Richardson, Cheryl. *Life Makeovers.* London: Bantam Books, Transworld Publishers, 2000

Richardson, Cheryl. *Take Time for Your Life.* New York: Random House, Inc., 1999

Robbins, Anthony. *Awaken the Giant Within.* New York: Summit Books, 1991

Roddick, Anita. *A Revolution in Kindness.* New York: HarperCollins, 2003

Roselle, Bruce E., Ph.D. *Vital Truths.* Edina, MN: Beaver's Pond Press, 2002

Ruiz, Don Miguel. *The Four Agreements.* San Rafael, CA: Amber-Allen Publishing, Inc., 1997

Spangler, Ann. *She Who Laughs, Lasts!* Grand Rapids, MI: Zondervan, 2000

Steil, Dr. Lyman K. & Dr. Richard K. Bommelje. *Listening Leaders: The Ten Golden Rules to Listen, Lead & Succeed.* Edina, MN: Beaver's Pond Press, 2004

Tolle, Eckhart. *The Power of Now.* Novato, CA: New World Library 1999

Vaughan, Frances E. *Awakening Intuition.* New York: St. Martin's Press, 1989

Vienne, Veronique. *The Art of Imperfection.* New York: Clarkson Potter/Publishers, 1999

Vineyard, Sue. *How to Take Care of You...So You Can Take Care of Others.* Downers Grove, IL: Heritage Arts Publishing, 1989

Vreeland, Nicholas. *An Open Heart: The Dalai Lama Practicing Compassion in Everyday Life.* New York: Time Warner Publishing, 2001

Wagner, David. *Life as a Daymaker: How to Change the World by Simply Making Someone's Day.* Carlsbad, CA: Hay House Inc., 2003

Waldman, Jackie. *The Courage to Give.* Berkeley, CA: Conari Press, 2001

Waldman, Jackie. *Teens with the Courage to Give.* Berkeley, CA: Conari Press, 2000

Warren, Rick. *The Purpose Driven Life.* Grand Rapids, MI: Zondervan, 2002

Weiss, Brian L., M.D. *Only Love Is Real.* New York: Warner Books, Inc., 1996

Williamson, Marianne. *Illuminata.* New York: The Berkley Publishing Group, 1994

Winfrey, Oprah. *O, The Oprah Magazine.* New York, NY: The Hearst Corporation. Oprah, Angel Network, Get with the Program, Harpo, Make the Connection, Oprah's Book Club, and Remembering your Spirit are registered trademarks of Harpo, Inc. Spa Girls, and Use Your Life, are trademarks of Harpo, Inc.

Zukav, Gary. *The Seat of the Soul.* New York: Simon & Schuster, 1990

Zukav, Gary. *Soul Stories.* New York: Simon & Schuster, 2000

Magazines/Newspapers/ Periodicals/Tapes/Websites

Challenge a Day: Challenging You to be the Change. Website: *www.challengeday.org*

Fishman, Jim. *AARP the Magazine*. Washington, D.C.: Press Images, March/April 2003

Harris, Joshua. New Attitude. Spring 1995 issue. Website: *newattitude@sovgracemin.org*

Highgate Dolls & Craft. Clarmont Ave., Highgate P.O., St. Mary Jamaica, WI. Phone: 876-724-1235. Website: *www.highgatedollsandcraft.com*

Lilja, Duane. Walls to Bridges: Contributing to Developing Civil Societies. Website: *www.wallstobridges.com*

Palmer, Stacy. *Washington-based Chronicle of Philanthropy*. February 2002–2003

Partners in Kindness Website: *www.partnersinkindness.org*

Passion In Action: Doing What You Love in Service to Humanity. Website: *www.passioninaction.org*

Robbins, Anthony. Motivational audio tapes: *A Thirty-day Program for Unlimited Success...Personal Power.*"

University of Michigan. *Psychological Science*. New York: Cambridge University Press, 2003

Wagner, David. *Life as a Daymaker*. Website: *www.daymaker.net*

Acknowledgments

I am deeply grateful to the many friends, students, parents, teachers, colleagues, and managers who have helped shape my life over the past three decades.

A special thanks to my seventh grade English teacher, Mrs. Allen, and my senior high Social Studies teacher, John O'Brien, from Centennial Junior and Senior High Schools in Circle Pines, Minnesota, who always had faith in me, acknowledged my writing talent, and encouraged me to continue.

I greatly appreciate the guidance of Gustavus Adolphus College Sociology Professor John Prehn who encouraged me to write my life story as a freshman. His outstanding remarks, along with exceptional grades bestowed, gave me the confidence to explore my writing skill. I would also like to thank Advanced Public Speaking Professor William Robertz whose intense brainpower challenged me like no other to truly absorb, learn, and adapt. His powerful intellect and firm teachings, which seemed grueling at the time, created who I am today and have helped bring out my greatest potential.

I have been deeply enriched by the brilliant insights of authors Julia Cameron, Wayne Dyer, Gary Zukav, Don Miguel Ruiz, Eckhart Tolle, Cheryl Richardson, and Dr. Phillip McGraw. Also thanks to Oprah Winfrey, Peace Pilgrim, and those all around the world who continue to live and give compassionately from their hearts and souls, striving to make our world a better place for all.

I thank my soul mates Dr. Kristen Brown, Dan McCormick and Greg Steerman for giving me the benefit of their life wisdom, which have broadened my thinking immeasurably. Also friends who have been a part of my growth and learning experience: Kristie Kripotos, Jan Prehn, Brenda Glatzmaier, Tina Hyland, Heather Reuss, Katrina Ritter Krueger, Julie Leither Redmond, Lucy Rosario, Geri LaFond, John Emery, Chad McKenney, Cindy Erdall, Dennis Kelly, and my dear friends from the first seven years of my life in an orphanage in Tehran, Iran: Susan Bruhmuller and Nilu.

I am forever grateful to my mom and dad for adopting me and giving me a chance to truly live. I cherish the bond with my sisters Shannon and Chau. I am thankful for Ron Card and his family for their joyful spirits and the many memorable dinner outings. Also thank you to my grandpa's wisdom, which allowed me to see that I was living commercially, mechanically, and topically. He taught me to see my inner self, my true good, and that what matters most to my soul and this world is what comes about naturally.

I appreciate the warm hearts and extreme kindness of Mary Kaye Golden, Peggy McCormick, and Patti Bjork. Also the Brown family: Jerry, Paula, Kelly, Holly, and Paul for their incredible support, creativity, and brilliant minds.

I am delighted by the extreme professionalism, generosity and goodwill of the Wally McCarthy's Cadillac, Inc. in Roseville, Minnesota. I especially have great admiration for the genuine support and service extended by Alix Jacques Moise. Also Sales Manager Bill Emstad for having faith in my book and kicking off my first book signing.

I also wish to thank the remarkable Christ Church Preschool Learning Center in Minneapolis for their generosity and thoughtfulness. Pastor Albert Neibacher, Jr.; Director Stephanie Gustafson; Stephanie Okoneski; Sue Dahl; and many parents and kids have filled my heart with joy. Special thanks to those who went out of their way with their warmth and support following my surgeries: Nancy and Andy Hokkanen;

Shannon, Jim, Cole, and Maddie Ferguson; Laurie, Mike, and Rachel Petruconis; Sarah and Brie Forster; Rose and Patric Carlsen; and Nancy and Maggie Schauff.

I'm fortunate to have worked with some very fine managers and business people: Owner of Desq Dennis McGraw, Marshall Field's Vice President Don Swanson, Store Manager Bill Peters, and Managers Rich Brewers and Dave Barton. Also Bruggeman Homes' New Home Specialist John Haselbeck.

I am grateful for the time, thoughts, and efforts extended by Richard Obershaw and Dennis and Claire Jandt.

I extend my most sincere gratitude to my dearest, closest "second" family: Debbie, Bart, Dylan, and Taylor Dabrowski along with MaryAnn Millay and Greg Morey. I could write a whole book on their kind acts. They are far and away the most authentic, good-natured people I've ever met, and I'm honored to have known them for half my life.

I have great appreciation for the time, effort and mind works of Milt Adams, Cindy Rogers, Judith Palmateer, Maria Girsch, and the Beaver's Pond Press publishing team in Edina, Minnesota. Also Jack Caravela, Jaana Bykonich, and designing team at Mori Studio in St. Anthony, Minnesota. They have contributed to making my dream a reality by bringing my Chosen Eulogy to life.

About the Author

Kian K. Dwyer

A spiritual mentor, speaker, writer, and twenty-year consultant, is redefining "kindness" by facilitating students, parents, and those in the workforce to uphold their true purpose in life. That means that they emanate their authentic values, giving from the heart and living with intention. Kian Dwyer is the founder of **World Help Organization** along with *Key on Giving* and *Key on Action* services which reintroduce kindness and promote active giving.

Through her speaking presentations and fundraising events, Ms. Dwyer collectively supports individuals who are ready to make a difference in the universe. Her book and business are not about "self-help," but "world-help," putting your best authentic self forward to better the world. It's not about the "weakest link," but about being your **best** strongest link in a chain with other leaders involved in transmitting a new, desired compassionate lifestyle. This ripple effect provides the energy for the creation of a world of kindness.

As Ms. Dwyer puts it, "Our country is still recovering from the tragedy of 9-11-2001. Let's not wait for another jolt of terror to become what we're meant to be. We each have something to offer. We can all be leaders and heroes by living from our goodness within, by being compassionate, giving, and kind to ourselves, others, and the universe every day."

Ms. Dwyer has volunteered for a number of organizations to help special-needs kids with autism, ADHD and fetal alcohol syndrome. She volunteers and does fundraising for several private schools, Children's Miracle Network, ALS, and the Breast Cancer Association.

She looks up to Oprah Winfrey and values her concept on *"acts of kindness"* through her Angel Network. Oprah is the leading link to redefining kindness in our world. Ms. Dwyer hopes to captivate many more leaders who may each passionately add their unique link of talents and gifts. She says, "There are no followers. We are all leaders, and each of us is indispensable. We each represent a critical link. The chain is a connection among the finest people actively showing possibilities through acts of kindness."

Ms. Dwyer holds a Bachelor of Arts degree in Speech/Communications with a minor in Psychology from Gustavus Adolphus College in St. Peter, Minnesota. She is an active participant and regular contributor for classes and workshops in development training for special-needs kids. She lives in the Twin Cities where she enjoys relaxing, reading, photography, and playing the piano. She can be reached by mail at World Help Organization, P.O. Box 75584 St. Paul, MN 55175. You can visit her website at *www.worldhelporganization.org.*